EASTER ISLAND
TRAVEL GUIDE 2025 AND BEYOND

A Journey Through Culture, Hidden Gems, Cuisine and Local Secrets of Rapa Nui in the Southeastern Pacific Ocean of Chile – Packed with Detailed Maps & Itinerary Planner

BY

JAMES W. PATRICK

Copyright © 2024 by James W. Patrick. All rights reserved. The content of this work, including but not limited to text, images, and other media, is owned by James W. Patrick and is protected under copyright laws and international agreements. No part of this work may be reproduced, shared, or transmitted in any form or by any means without the explicit written consent of James W. Patrick. Unauthorized use, duplication, or distribution of this material may lead to legal action, including both civil and criminal penalties. For permission requests or further inquiries, please reach out to the author via the contact details provided in the book or on the author's official page.

TABLE OF CONTENTS

Copyright 1
My Experience in Easter Island 5
Benefits of this Guide 7

Chapter 1: Introduction to Easter Island 11
1.1 Welcome to Easter Island 11
1.2 History and Mystery 12
1.3 Geography and Climate 13
1.4 Getting to Easter Island 14
1.5 Easter Island for First Time Travelers 15

Chapter 2: Accommodation Options 17
2.1 Luxury Hotels and Resorts 18
2.2 Budget-Friendly Options 20
2.3 Vacation Rentals and Guesthouses 21
2.4 Camping on Easter Island 23
2.6 Boutique Hotels 25
2.7 Unique Stays: Eco-Lodges and Island Bungalows 27

Chapter 3: Transportation 30
3.1 Getting Around Easter Island 30
3.2 Public Transportation Options 31
3.3 Car Rentals and Driving Tips 32
3.4 Cycling and Walking on Easter Island 33
3.5 Shuttle Services 35

Chapter 4: Top 10 Attractions & Hidden Gems 38
4.1 Moai Statues 39
4.2 Rano Raraku Volcano 41
4.3 Anakena Beach 43

4.4 Orongo Birdman Cult Site...45

4.5 Ahu Tongariki..47

4.6 Easter Island National Park..50

4.7 Caves of Easter Island..51

4.8 Easter Island Museum...53

4.9 Hanga Roa Town..56

4.10 Ovahe Beach..58

4.11 Outdoor Activities and Adventures..59

4.12 Guided Tours and Recommended Tour Operators...................61

Chapter 5 Practical Information and Guidance...................................63

5.1 Maps and Navigation...63

5.2 Five Days Itinerary..65

5.3 Essential Packing List..68

5.4 Setting Your Travel Budget..70

5.5 Visa Requirements and Entry Procedures....................................71

5.6 Safety Tips and Emergency Contacts...73

5.7 Currency Exchange and Banking Services...................................74

5.8 Language, Communication and Useful Phrases.........................76

5.9 Shopping on Easter Island...79

5.10 Health and Wellness Centers..81

5.11 Useful Websites, Mobile Apps and Online Resources..............83

5.12 Internet Access and Connectivity...85

5.13 Visitor Centers and Tourist Assistance..87

Chapter 6: Gastronomic Delights..90

6.1 Dining Options and Top Restaurants..90

6.2 Cafes and Food Trucks...93

6.3 Cooking Classes and Culinary Tours...94

6.4 Traditional Easter Island Cuisine...97

6.5 Local Markets and Street Food...99

6.6 Wine Bars and Nightlife...101

Chapter 7: Day Trips and Excursions...103
7.1 Island Hopping... 103
7.2 Scuba Diving and Snorkeling...106
7.3 Easter Island Hiking Trails...108
7.4 Horseback Riding.. 111
7.5 Exploring Easter Island's Hidden Coves... 113

Chapter 8: Events and Festivals... 116
8.1 Tapati Festival... 116
8.2 Easter Island Music Festival..119
8.3 Island Clean-Up Initiative... 121
8.4 Cultural Heritage Day... 124
8.5 Christmas on Easter Island.. 127
Insider Tips and Recommendations.. 129

MY EXPERIENCE IN EASTER ISLAND

Easter Island, or Rapa Nui as its indigenous inhabitants call it, is a place where time seems to pause, offering an unparalleled experience that lingers long after departure. From the moment my plane touched down on the small runway of Mataveri International Airport, I was greeted by the island's serene beauty and the warm, welcoming smiles of the locals. The island's small size, just 63 square miles, made every corner feel intimately accessible, while its isolation in the vast Pacific Ocean added to the allure of its remote charm. The hospitality of the Rapa Nui people immediately enveloped me, embodying the island's deep-rooted traditions of openness and generosity. At the heart of Easter Island's enchantment are the Moai statues, colossal stone figures that stand as silent sentinels of a bygone era. Each statue, some weighing over 80 tons, holds a mysterious allure that captivates visitors. My visit to Ahu Tongariki, the island's largest Moai platform, was particularly unforgettable. As the sun dipped below the horizon, casting a golden glow over the statues, I was struck by the grandeur and solemnity of these ancient figures. The Moai seemed to whisper tales of an ancient civilization that once thrived here, their silent presence evoking a deep sense of reverence and connection to the past.

Exploring Rano Raraku, the volcanic quarry where the Moai were sculpted, was like stepping into a living museum. This surreal landscape, dotted with partially finished statues and remnants of ancient craftsmanship, offered a rare glimpse into the monumental effort behind the Moai's creation. The silence of the quarry, broken only by the distant cries of seabirds, added to the feeling of timelessness and isolation. Standing among these unfinished statues, I felt a profound appreciation for the Rapa Nui people's ingenuity and dedication. The journey to Orongo, a ceremonial village perched on the rim of the Rano Kau crater, took me further into the island's mystical history. Orongo was the center of the Birdman cult, and the archaeological remains of this ceremonial site offered insights into the complex rituals and competitions that were once held here. The panoramic views from Orongo, with the crater lake below and the rocky islets of Motu Nui, Motu Iti, and Motu Kao Kao in the distance, were nothing short of breathtaking. The legend of the Birdman competition and the spiritual significance of this site added a deeper layer to my understanding of Rapa Nui's cultural heritage.

Beyond its historical and cultural treasures, Easter Island is a haven of natural beauty. The island's beaches, such as Anakena, offer pristine white sand and crystal-clear waters, perfect for a relaxing swim or a leisurely stroll. The contrast between the island's lush greenery and the deep blue of the Pacific Ocean created a stunning backdrop for moments of reflection and tranquility. As I explored the island's diverse landscapes, from rugged volcanic terrain to serene coastal vistas, I found solace in the natural beauty that complemented the island's rich cultural tapestry. Leaving Easter Island was a poignant experience, tinged with a bittersweet sense of departure. The island's mystique, the warmth of its people, and the grandeur of its Moai statues had woven themselves into the fabric of my memories. As the plane ascended and the island's rugged beauty receded into the distance, I felt a deep sense of gratitude for having experienced such an extraordinary place. Easter Island is not merely a destination; it is a timeless journey into a world of ancient wonder and natural splendor, offering an adventure that resonates deeply and lingers long after one has left its shores.

BENEFITS OF THIS GUIDE

As you prepare to venture to this isolated paradise, this guide will provide a thorough overview of everything you need to know, from navigating its rugged terrain to immersing yourself in its unique cultural tapestry. Whether you're drawn by the mystical Moai statues, the island's vibrant culture, or its breathtaking natural beauty, this guide aims to equip you with the knowledge to make your journey as enriching and seamless as possible.

Maps and Navigation: Navigating Easter Island, despite its small size, requires thoughtful preparation due to its limited infrastructure. The guide includes detailed maps that outline key landmarks, including the iconic Moai statues, volcanic craters, and picturesque beaches. To complement these maps, we provide advice on both offline and digital navigation options, such as GPS devices and mobile apps, ensuring that you can find your way whether you're exploring the island's rugged paths or its charming coastal roads. Given the island's limited mobile coverage, having a reliable paper map on hand will be particularly useful for staying oriented during your adventures. This comprehensive navigation section will help you confidently traverse the island and discover its many wonders.

Accommodation Options: Easter Island offers a diverse range of accommodation options to suit various preferences and budgets. From opulent resorts like Explora Rapa Nui and Hangaroa Eco Village & Spa, which provide unparalleled luxury and breathtaking views, to more affordable mid-range hotels such as Hotel Puku Vai and Hotel Hare Uta, which balance comfort and convenience, there is something for every traveler. Budget-conscious visitors will find cozy hostels and guesthouses like Taha Tai and Cabañas Moai, offering a more economical stay while still providing a unique island experience. For those seeking a more homely environment, vacation rentals are available, catering to families or groups looking for a private retreat. This guide ensures that you can find the perfect place to rest after a day of exploration.

Transportation: Getting around Easter Island is relatively straightforward due to its small size, though transportation options are limited. Renting a car is highly recommended for those who wish to explore independently, as it allows for flexible travel across the island's varied terrain. For a more leisurely pace, scooters and bicycles are available for rent, providing a relaxed way to enjoy the island's scenic routes. Public transportation consists primarily of local buses, but these can be infrequent and limited in coverage. Taxis are also an option, though they can be costly. Many visitors opt for guided tours, which not only provide transportation but also offer valuable insights into the island's history and culture. This guide will help you choose the best transportation options to enhance your island experience.

Top Attractions: Easter Island is renowned for its remarkable historical and cultural landmarks, each offering a unique glimpse into its rich heritage. The island's most iconic attractions are the Moai statues, colossal stone figures that embody the island's ancient spirit. Sites such as Ahu Tongariki, Rano Raraku, and Ahu Akivi are essential visits for anyone interested in the Moai's fascinating history and significance. Additionally, the volcanic crater of Rano Kau and the ancient village of Orongo provide stunning panoramic views and insights into traditional Rapa Nui practices. Anakena Beach, with its golden sands and historical Moai statues, offers a perfect blend of relaxation and exploration. The Museo Antropológico Sebastián Englert in Hanga Roa further enriches your visit with its extensive collection of artifacts and exhibits. This guide details these attractions to ensure you experience the best of what Easter Island has to offer.

Practical Information and Travel Resources: Understanding practical aspects of traveling to Easter Island is crucial for a smooth and enjoyable trip. Most travelers will need a valid passport and may require a visa, depending on their nationality, so it is essential to check with the Chilean consulate for up-to-date entry requirements. Health precautions, such as drinking bottled water and using sunscreen, are advisable due to the island's remote location and strong sun exposure. Familiarizing yourself with local emergency contacts, including medical facilities and police numbers, will ensure you are prepared for any unforeseen circumstances. Respecting local customs and traditions is also important; always seek permission before photographing sacred sites and follow guidelines provided by local authorities. This guide provides all the necessary practical information to help you navigate these aspects effectively.

Culinary Delights: Easter Island's culinary scene is a delightful fusion of Polynesian flavors and modern influences. Local specialties, such as Po'e, a sweet pumpkin dessert, and Ceviche, featuring fresh seafood marinated in citrus, offer a taste of the island's unique gastronomic culture. Dining options on the island cater to a range of tastes, from upscale restaurants like Te Moana and

Kaloa, which provide exquisite international and local dishes, to casual eateries such as Club Sandwich and La Kaleta, which offer a relaxed dining experience. Additionally, exploring local markets for fresh produce and street food provides an authentic glimpse into everyday island life. This guide highlights the best dining experiences to ensure you savor every aspect of Easter Island's vibrant food scene.

Culture and Heritage: Easter Island's culture and heritage are deeply rooted in its Polynesian history, offering visitors a rich and immersive experience. Traditional festivals and ceremonies provide an opportunity to witness Rapa Nui music, dance, and rituals firsthand. The island's art and crafts, including traditional carvings and woven goods, reflect its rich cultural heritage and are available for purchase in local galleries and shops. While Spanish is the official language, many locals also speak Rapa Nui, the indigenous language, and learning a few basic phrases can enhance your cultural interactions. This guide delves into the island's cultural practices and traditions, helping you engage meaningfully with the local community and appreciate its heritage.

Outdoor Activities and Adventures: For outdoor enthusiasts, Easter Island offers a range of activities that showcase its natural beauty and rugged terrain. Hiking trails around Rano Kau and other volcanic craters provide stunning vistas and a chance to explore the island's diverse landscapes. Snorkeling and diving in the island's clear waters reveal vibrant marine life and underwater marvels. For those looking for a unique way to explore the island, horseback riding tours offer an adventurous perspective on the terrain. This guide provides detailed information on these outdoor activities, ensuring that you can fully enjoy the island's natural offerings.

Shopping: Shopping on Easter Island is an opportunity to find unique souvenirs and local goods that capture the island's essence. Souvenir shops in Hanga Roa offer a variety of items, from Moai replicas to handcrafted Rapa Nui art. Local markets are also a great place to discover traditional crafts, including woven baskets, carvings, and jewelry. These keepsakes not only serve as mementos of your trip but also support local artisans. This guide helps you navigate the island's shopping scene, ensuring you can find meaningful and authentic souvenirs to remember your visit.

Day Trips and Excursions: Exploring Easter Island beyond its main attractions offers additional layers of discovery. Day trips to sites like Rano Raraku, where Moai statues were carved, and Ahu Tongariki, home to the island's largest group of Moai, provide deeper insights into the island's history. Excursions to the surrounding islets, or motus, offer pristine beaches and exceptional snorkeling opportunities. These additional activities and excursions expand your experience, allowing you to explore lesser-known areas and fully appreciate the island's diverse offerings. This guide includes recommendations for day trips and excursions to ensure you make the most of your time on Easter Island.

Entertainment and Nightlife: Easter Island's entertainment and nightlife scene, while more subdued compared to urban destinations, offers a unique local flavor. Local bars and cafés, such as the Club Social y Cultural Rapa Nui, provide a relaxed atmosphere where you can enjoy live music and cultural performances. Traditional dance and music shows, often organized by hotels and cultural centers, offer an immersive experience into Rapa Nui's vibrant artistic traditions. This guide highlights the best places and events for evening entertainment, ensuring that you can enjoy the island's nightlife and cultural expressions.

CHAPTER 1
INTRODUCTION TO EASTER ISLAND

1.1 Welcome to Easter Island

Imagine a place so remote that it feels as though it exists at the edge of the world. Easter Island, also known as Rapa Nui, is precisely this enigmatic destination, a speck of land in the vast expanse of the Pacific Ocean. Located about 3,700 kilometers west of Chile, it sits isolated, a solitary island surrounded by the endless blue. Despite its isolation, it has captured the imagination of explorers and travelers from around the globe. As you approach Easter Island, you are greeted by its remarkable landscape, a blend of volcanic craters, verdant hills, and dramatic coastlines. The island's most famous feature, the Moai statues, stand as silent sentinels watching over the land. These colossal figures, with their solemn faces and oversized heads, are not just art; they are the heart of a mystery that has intrigued historians and travelers alike. Easter Island's charm lies not just in its physical beauty but in its aura of mystery. The Moai statues, created by the Rapa Nui people between 1400 and 1650 AD, seem to whisper secrets of an ancient civilization. Each statue represents an important ancestor, believed to have spiritual power and influence. As you walk among these statues, you can't help but feel a deep sense of connection to the past, an almost tangible link to the people who once inhabited this remote land.

The island's small capital, Hanga Roa, serves as a welcoming point for visitors. Here, you will find a blend of local culture and modern convenience. The charming town offers a glimpse into the daily life of the Rapa Nui people, with local markets, traditional dance performances, and delicious Polynesian cuisine. The sense of community is palpable, and the warm hospitality of the locals makes every visitor feel like a cherished guest. The allure of Easter Island extends beyond its physical attributes. It is a place where the natural world and human history intersect in profound ways. Every sunrise and sunset here seems to carry a special significance, illuminating the Moai statues and casting shadows that enhance their mystique. Every corner of the island tells a story, inviting you to explore and uncover its many secrets. A visit to Easter Island is not merely a trip; it is an immersive experience that offers a rare opportunity to connect with one of the world's most isolated and intriguing destinations.

1.2 History and Mystery

Easter Island's history is as enigmatic as its Moai statues. The island, discovered by Dutch explorer Jacob Roggeveen on Easter Sunday in 1722, was already a place of rich cultural and historical significance. The Rapa Nui people, who had settled on the island long before European contact, developed a complex society and an impressive array of monuments, the most notable of which are the Moai statues. The origin of the Rapa Nui people remains a subject of fascination and debate. It is believed that they arrived from Polynesia, navigating the vast Pacific Ocean using sophisticated navigational techniques. Their arrival marked the beginning of a vibrant culture characterized by complex social structures and intricate artistry. The construction of the Moai statues began in this period, serving as both a tribute to ancestors and a symbol of the spiritual power believed to be vested in these monumental figures.

The Moai statues themselves are a testament to the Rapa Nui's ingenuity and dedication. Carved from volcanic tuff, these statues were painstakingly transported across the island, often from quarries to their ceremonial sites. The process involved significant community effort and reflected the deep cultural importance of these statues. They were placed on stone platforms called Ahu, which served as both a shrine and a place of worship. The Ahu are often found along the coast, overlooking the sea, which adds to the mystical aura surrounding them. Over the centuries, the island faced significant challenges, including internal conflicts, resource depletion, and external influences. The arrival of Europeans brought new pressures and led to dramatic changes in Rapa

Nui society. Despite these challenges, the Rapa Nui people have preserved their cultural heritage, and the Moai statues remain a powerful symbol of their enduring legacy. Today, the Moai statues are not just relics of the past but living symbols of a culture that continues to thrive. They represent a link between the past and the present, offering a glimpse into the lives of the Rapa Nui ancestors and inviting visitors to ponder the mysteries of their creation and purpose. Easter Island's history is woven with threads of intrigue and wonder, making it a destination that both captivates and challenges the imagination.

1.3 Geography and Climate

Covering an area of around 163.6 square kilometers, the island is known for its volcanic origins, which have sculpted its distinct landscape. The island features three primary volcanic craters: Rano Kau, Rano Raraku, and Poike. These craters, along with other volcanic formations, create a diverse terrain of rolling hills, rugged coastlines, and verdant valleys. Rano Raraku is particularly notable as the site where the famous Moai statues were carved, providing a deep connection to the island's cultural heritage. The coastal areas of Easter Island offer breathtaking views of the Pacific Ocean, with numerous trails and paths leading to some of the island's most renowned landmarks. Navigating this varied geography is both a challenge and a delight, enhancing the island's appeal as a travel destination.

Climate Overview of Easter Island

Easter Island enjoys a subtropical climate that remains relatively mild and pleasant throughout the year. However, the island experiences two distinct seasons that influence the best times to visit: the wet season and the dry season.

Wet Season: The wet season, spanning from April to September, is characterized by cooler temperatures and increased rainfall. During this period, temperatures generally range from 18°C to 24°C (64°F to 75°F). Rainfall is more frequent, which enhances the island's lush, green scenery. Despite the occasional downpour, the rain typically comes in short bursts, leaving ample time for exploring the island's natural and cultural attractions. The cooler temperatures during this season make outdoor activities more comfortable, and the reduced number of tourists often results in a more peaceful visit. This period provides an opportunity to enjoy the island's beauty without the bustle of peak tourist traffic.

Dry Season: The dry season, from October to March, brings warmer temperatures and lower humidity to Easter Island. Daytime temperatures during these months range between 22°C and 28°C (72°F to 82°F). This season is characterized by drier conditions, with significantly less rainfall compared to the wet season. The lower humidity and warmer temperatures create ideal conditions for outdoor activities, making it a popular time for tourists. The dry season is also the time when the island experiences its highest influx of visitors, which can mean busier attractions and higher prices for accommodations and services.

Best Times to Visit: Choosing the best time to visit Easter Island depends on personal preferences and travel goals. The wet season offers a quieter experience with lush landscapes, while the dry season provides optimal weather for exploring and enjoying outdoor activities. Both seasons have their own unique charm, and the choice largely depends on whether you prefer cooler, less crowded conditions or warmer, more active periods. Overall, Easter Island's climate is one of its many appealing features, offering diverse experiences year-round. Whether you visit during the serene wet season or the vibrant dry season, you are sure to find a captivating and memorable experience on this remarkable island.

1.4 Getting to Easter Island

There are no direct train or road routes to Easter Island due to its placement in the vast Pacific Ocean, air travel remains the most viable and straightforward method to reach this captivating destination. Below, you will find comprehensive information on the best ways to get to Easter Island, including details on airlines, ticketing, and essential travel tips.

Arriving by Air Travel: The primary gateway to Easter Island is Mataveri International Airport (IPC), situated near the island's main town, Hanga Roa. LATAM Airlines is the principal carrier providing regular flights to the island. LATAM operates direct flights from Santiago, Chile, to Easter Island, with a flight duration of approximately five hours. Santiago is a major hub, and LATAM's flights to Easter Island are well-integrated into their network, making the journey accessible for international travelers. For those planning their visit, LATAM Airlines offers a range of ticketing options. Prices for one-way flights typically range from $500 to $800 USD, depending on the season and how far in advance you book. To secure the best rates, it is advisable to book your flight several months in advance. You can explore flight schedules, compare prices, and make reservations directly through LATAM's official website (https://www.latam.com). Additionally, you might find competitive fares through online travel agencies such as (https://www.expedia.com) or (https://www.kayak.com).

Practical Travel Considerations: Traveling to Easter Island involves more than just booking a flight. Given its remoteness, it is crucial to check for any specific entry requirements or travel advisories that might affect your journey. These details are typically available on official Chilean government websites or through LATAM Airlines. Ensure that your passport is valid for at least six months beyond your intended departure date, and consider purchasing travel insurance to cover any unforeseen circumstances. Upon arrival at Mataveri International Airport, travelers will find a modest but functional facility. Transportation options, including taxis and shuttle services provided by local hotels, are available to take you to Hanga Roa and various accommodations. The island's small size means that most attractions and lodgings are easily accessible from the airport.

1.5 Easter Island for First Time Travelers

By preparing thoughtfully and approaching your visit with an open mind, you can make the most of your time on Easter Island. Embrace its unique offerings, respect its cultural and environmental significance, and enjoy an unforgettable journey into one of the world's most fascinating destinations.

Embrace the Mystique of the Moai Statues: As you explore Easter Island, understanding the significance of the Moai statues is crucial. These monumental figures are not merely historical relics but represent a profound aspect of Rapa Nui culture and spirituality. The Moai, sculpted from volcanic tuff and placed on ceremonial platforms called Ahu, were once integral to the island's social and religious practices. When visiting sites such as Rano Raraku, the quarry where many of these statues were carved, and Ahu Tongariki, known for its impressive lineup of Moai, take time to reflect on their cultural importance and the stories they embody. Approach these statues with respect and curiosity to fully appreciate their historical and spiritual significance.

Plan Your Journey and Accommodations: Given the island's remote location, planning ahead is essential. Easter Island is situated approximately 3,700 kilometers west of Chile, requiring a flight from Santiago that takes about 5 hours. Due to its isolation, flight and accommodation options can be limited, so it is advisable to book your travel and lodging well in advance. The island offers a range of accommodations from budget to luxury, but early reservations ensure that you find a place that fits your needs and preferences.

Pack for Varied Weather Conditions: Easter Island's weather can be unpredictable, with sudden rain showers and strong sunlight. To stay comfortable while exploring, pack lightweight, breathable clothing for the warm days, but also bring a rain jacket to protect against unexpected showers. Sun protection, including sunscreen, a hat, and sunglasses, is important due to the island's strong UV rays. Additionally, comfortable walking shoes are a must, as many of the island's attractions involve walking over uneven terrain.

Respect Local Customs and Preservation Efforts: Easter Island is a place of deep cultural significance and environmental sensitivity. To ensure that future generations can also enjoy its wonders, it's important to respect local customs and adhere to conservation guidelines. Avoid touching or climbing on the Moai statues and follow all posted signs and regulations. By being considerate of the island's cultural and environmental heritage, you contribute to its preservation and help maintain the respect that the Rapa Nui people have for their history and land.

Engage with the Local Community: One of the most enriching aspects of visiting Easter Island is the opportunity to engage with its local community. The Rapa Nui people are known for their hospitality and friendliness. Participate in local cultural activities, such as traditional dance performances or craft workshops, to gain a deeper understanding of the island's culture. This interaction not only enhances your experience but also fosters a meaningful connection with the island's residents and their traditions.

CHAPTER 2
ACCOMMODATION OPTIONS

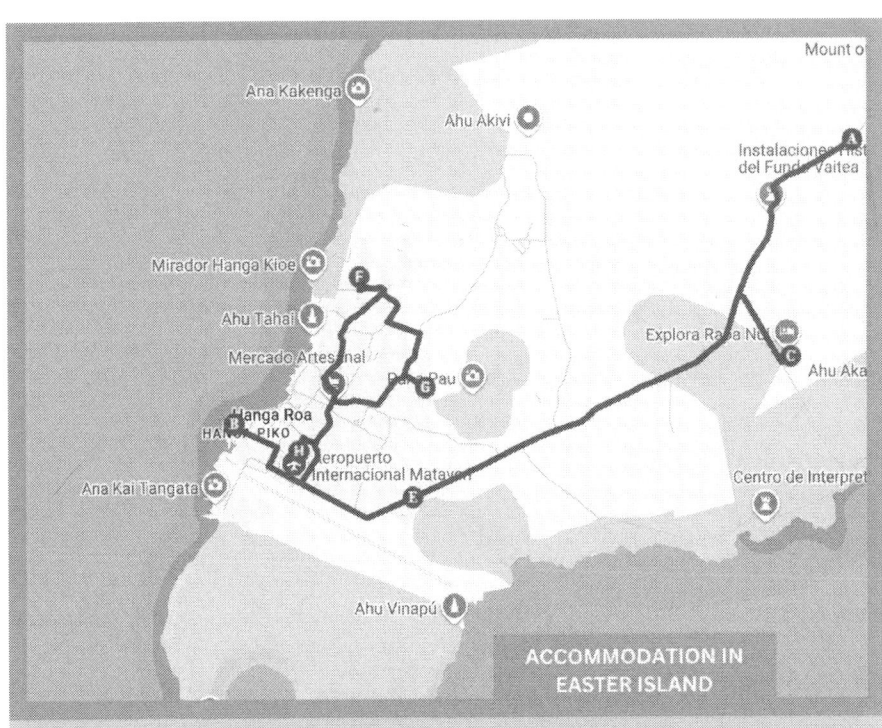

ACCOMMODATION IN EASTER ISLAND

Directions from Easter Island, Chile to CABAÑAS CHRISTOPHE - Policarpo Toro, Hanga Roa, Easter Island, Chile

A Easter Island, Chile	**D** Nayara Hangaroa - Pont, Hanga Roa, Easter Island, Chile	**G** Hostal Pukao, Hanga Roa, Easter Island, Chile
B Hangaroa Eco Village & Spa - Pont, Hanga Roa, Easter Island, Chile	**E** Hotel Hare Uta - CAMINO A ANAKENA, Valparaíso, Easter Island, Chile	**H** Kona Tau Hostelling, Hanga Roa, Easter Island, Chile
C Explora Rapa Nui, Hanga Roa, Easter Island, Chile	**F** Hotel Altiplanico Rapa Nui, Easter Island, Chile	**I** CABAÑAS CHRISTOPHE - Policarpo Toro, Hanga Roa, Easter Island, Chile

2.1 Luxury Hotels and Resorts

Easter Island offers more than just a journey through history. For those seeking an experience of refined luxury, the island presents a selection of exquisite hotels and resorts that blend opulence with the island's unique allure. Located within its secluded landscapes, these accommodations offer a perfect retreat for discerning travelers who desire not only comfort but also a deep connection with the island's mystical charm. Each luxury establishment on Easter Island is a gateway to lavish amenities, world-class services, and an intimate encounter with the breathtaking beauty of the Pacific.

Hangaroa Eco Village & Spa: Located on the southwestern coast of Easter Island, the Hangaroa Eco Village & Spa stands as a testament to sustainable luxury. This five-star resort offers a harmonious blend of modern design and traditional Rapa Nui architecture, creating a serene environment that is both eco-friendly and indulgent. Guests are welcomed into spacious, elegantly designed rooms that feature natural materials and breathtaking ocean views. With prices starting around $600 per night, this resort provides a full suite of amenities including a world-class spa, infinity pool, and gourmet dining options that highlight local flavors. Unique to Hangaroa is its commitment to cultural immersion, offering guests tailored experiences such as guided tours to the island's archaeological sites. For more information and reservations, visitors can explore their official website (https://www.hangaroa.cl).

Explora Rapa Nui: Explora Rapa Nui, situated on a secluded hillside overlooking the vast Pacific, redefines the concept of luxury with its all-inclusive packages that start at approximately $1,300 per night. The resort's architecture seamlessly integrates with the surrounding landscape, providing guests with panoramic views of the ocean and the island's iconic moai. Rooms are designed to be sanctuaries of relaxation, with large windows that invite the natural beauty inside. The resort offers a unique blend of adventure and comfort, with guided excursions that include hiking, biking, and snorkeling, all tailored to immerse guests in the island's natural and cultural wonders. After a day of exploration, guests can unwind at the resort's exclusive spa, which offers treatments inspired by Polynesian traditions. More details can be found on their official website (https://www.explora.com/easter-island/).

Nayara Hangaroa: Nayara Hangaroa, positioned close to the main town of Hanga Roa, offers a luxurious escape with a focus on wellness and tranquility.

Prices start at around $750 per night, making it an exclusive option for those looking for both comfort and seclusion. The resort's design draws inspiration from the island's natural environment, with each room offering private terraces and luxurious amenities such as rain showers and premium bedding. Nayara's standout feature is its wellness center, which includes a range of spa treatments, a yoga pavilion, and wellness programs tailored to rejuvenate the body and spirit. Guests can indulge in gourmet cuisine at the resort's restaurant, which focuses on locally sourced ingredients and Rapa Nui culinary traditions. Booking details and further information are available on their official website (https://www.nayarahangaroa.com).

Hotel Hare Uta: Hotel Hare Uta, located amidst the rolling hills of Easter Island, is a boutique luxury hotel that offers a more intimate experience. With prices starting at around $500 per night, this hotel provides an exclusive retreat where guests can enjoy the privacy of individual bungalows, each designed with a mix of contemporary and traditional elements. The hotel's amenities include a spa, a garden with native plants, and a restaurant that serves a fusion of international and Rapa Nui cuisine. What sets Hotel Hare Uta apart is its commitment to sustainability, with initiatives that include organic farming and energy-efficient practices. The serene environment, combined with personalized services, makes it a perfect choice for travelers seeking peace and luxury. Additional details can be found on their official website (https://www.hareuta.com).

Altiplanico Rapa Nui: Altiplanico Rapa Nui, perched on a hillside with sweeping views of the Pacific Ocean, offers a luxurious yet laid-back experience that is perfect for those looking to connect with the island's natural beauty. Priced at around $400 per night, this hotel features rooms designed as independent bungalows, each with a private terrace that offers stunning ocean views. The hotel's infinity pool, surrounded by lush gardens, provides a perfect spot for relaxation, while the on-site restaurant offers a delectable menu of local and international dishes. Altiplanico's unique feature is its emphasis on blending with the environment, with architecture that mirrors the island's traditional Rapa Nui houses. Guests can explore more on their official website (https://www.altiplanico.com).

2.2 Budget-Friendly Options

Easter Island also offers a range of budget-friendly accommodations that provide comfort without compromising on the island's enchanting experience. For travelers looking to explore the mysteries of Rapa Nui without breaking the bank, these options offer cozy lodging, essential amenities, and the warm hospitality of the island's residents. From guesthouses to charming inns, Easter Island's budget-friendly accommodations ensure that every traveler can find a place to rest and rejuvenate after a day of exploring the island's rich cultural heritage.

Hostal Pukao: Hostal Pukao, located a short drive from the town center of Hanga Roa, offers an affordable and homely stay for travelers. Priced at around $80 per night, this guesthouse is known for its warm hospitality and personalized service. The rooms are simple yet comfortable, featuring private bathrooms, free Wi-Fi, and a shared kitchen for guests who prefer to prepare their meals. Hostal Pukao also offers free transportation to and from the airport, making it a convenient option for budget-conscious travelers. The lush garden and tranquil surroundings create a peaceful atmosphere, ideal for relaxation after a day of exploring. For reservations and more information, visitors can check their official website (https://www.hostalpukao.com).

Kona Tau Hostel: Kona Tau Hostel, situated in the heart of Hanga Roa, provides budget-friendly accommodation with a vibrant and social atmosphere. With prices starting at around $50 per night for a dormitory bed and $100 for a private room, Kona Tau is a popular choice among backpackers and solo travelers. The hostel offers basic amenities such as free breakfast, Wi-Fi, and a communal kitchen, fostering a sense of community among guests. What makes Kona Tau unique is its location, just a short walk from shops, restaurants, and the beach, making it an ideal base for exploring the island. For more details, bookings can be made through their website (https://www.konatauhostel.com).

Cabanas Christophe: Cabanas Christophe, located near the Rano Kau volcano, offers a charming and affordable option for those seeking a more private stay. Prices start at around $120 per night for a cabin, which includes a fully equipped kitchen, free Wi-Fi, and a private terrace with garden views. This accommodation is particularly suited for couples or small families who prefer the convenience of self-catering. Cabanas Christophe also offers a car rental service, allowing guests to explore the island at their own pace. The friendly staff provides personalized service, ensuring that guests feel at home during their stay. More information and reservations can be found on their official website (https://www.cabanaschristophe.com).

Hotel Victoria: Hotel Victoria, centrally located in Hanga Roa, offers value and convenience at a budget-friendly price of approximately $90 per night. The hotel features clean and comfortable rooms, each equipped with a private bathroom, air conditioning, and a mini-fridge. Guests can enjoy a complimentary breakfast each morning, and the hotel's location provides easy access to nearby shops, restaurants, and cultural sites. Hotel Victoria's friendly staff is always ready to assist with tour bookings and recommendations, ensuring that guests have a memorable experience on the island. Further details are available on their official website (https://www.hotelvictoria.cl).

Chez Steve Residence Kyle Mio: Chez Steve Residence Kyle Mio, offering a relaxed and welcoming environment, is a great choice for budget travelers. Located within walking distance of Hanga Roa's main attractions, this guesthouse offers rooms starting at around $70 per night. Each room is equipped with basic amenities, including a private bathroom and free Wi-Fi. Guests can enjoy a continental breakfast each morning and take advantage of the outdoor seating area to relax in the island's warm climate. The host, Steve, is known for his hospitality, offering guests insider tips on the best local spots to visit. For bookings and additional information, visitors can explore their official website (https://www.chezsteve.com).

2.3 Vacation Rentals and Guesthouses

For travelers seeking a more personalized and immersive experience on Easter Island, vacation rentals and guesthouses offer an ideal alternative to traditional hotel stays. These accommodations provide a home-away-from-home atmosphere, where guests can enjoy the freedom and flexibility of self-catering, coupled with the warmth and authenticity of staying with local hosts. Whether nestled in the heart of Hanga Roa or tucked away in serene, rural settings, these options offer a unique opportunity to experience the island's culture and natural beauty at a more intimate level.

Hare o Ahani: Hare o Ahani, a charming vacation rental located on the outskirts of Hanga Roa, offers a serene retreat for travelers seeking privacy and tranquility. This beautifully designed house features two bedrooms, a fully equipped kitchen, and a spacious living area, making it ideal for families or small groups. With prices starting at approximately $150 per night, Hare o Ahani offers great value for those looking to experience Easter Island at their own pace. The property is surrounded by lush gardens, providing a peaceful environment for relaxation. Guests can also enjoy amenities such as free Wi-Fi, a barbecue area, and complimentary airport transfers. For more information and reservations, visitors can check the website (https://www.hareoahani.com).

Cabanas Hinariru Nui: Cabanas Hinariru Nui, located in the tranquil area of Mataveri, offers a collection of traditional-style cabins that provide an authentic Rapa Nui experience. Each cabin is equipped with modern conveniences such as a kitchenette, private bathroom, and outdoor seating area, with prices starting around $100 per night. The cabins are designed to reflect the island's cultural heritage, with rustic furnishings and local artwork adorning the interiors. Guests can enjoy the peaceful surroundings and the close proximity to the island's main attractions, including the Orongo Ceremonial Village and the Rano Kau volcano. The host family is known for their warm hospitality, often providing guests with insights into the island's history and traditions. More details and bookings can be made through their official website (https://www.cabanashinariunui.com).

Maunga Roa Eco Lodge: Maunga Roa Eco Lodge, perched on a hillside with panoramic views of the Pacific Ocean, offers a luxurious yet eco-friendly vacation rental experience. The lodge features spacious accommodations, including private bungalows with fully equipped kitchens, large living areas, and private terraces. Prices start at approximately $200 per night, offering excellent value for travelers seeking both comfort and sustainability. The lodge's eco-friendly practices include solar power, rainwater harvesting, and organic gardening, making it an ideal choice for environmentally conscious travelers. Guests can also enjoy amenities such as free Wi-Fi, daily housekeeping, and guided tours of the island's natural and cultural sites. For more information and reservations, visitors can check the official website (https://www.maungaroaecolodge.com).

Residencial Vaianny: Residencial Vaianny, located in the heart of Hanga Roa, offers a quaint and affordable guesthouse experience. This family-run establishment provides cozy rooms with private bathrooms, starting at around $70 per night. The guesthouse is known for its warm, homely atmosphere, where guests are treated like family. A complimentary breakfast is served each morning, and guests have access to a communal kitchen and garden area. Residencial Vaianny's central location makes it a convenient base for exploring the island's attractions, with shops, restaurants, and cultural sites just a short walk away. The owners are always on hand to offer advice on the best places to visit and can assist with booking tours and activities. More information and bookings are available on their official website (https://www.residencialvaianny.com).

Cabanas Anavai Rapa Nui: Cabanas Anavai Rapa Nui, situated near the coastal area of Tahai, offers a cozy and comfortable vacation rental option for travelers. The property features individual cabins with prices starting at around $110 per night, each equipped with a kitchenette, private bathroom, and outdoor seating area. The cabins are surrounded by a beautiful garden, providing a peaceful setting for guests to relax and enjoy the island's natural beauty. Cabanas Anavai Rapa Nui is ideally located close to the famous Tahai archaeological site, offering guests easy access to one of the island's most iconic landmarks. The friendly hosts are known for their warm welcome and are happy to provide recommendations on local attractions and dining options. For more information and reservations, visitors can check the official website (https://www.cabanasanavai.com).

2.4 Camping on Easter Island

Easter Island offers a unique opportunity to connect with nature through camping. The island's campgrounds are not only budget-friendly but also provide an immersive experience, allowing visitors to wake up to the sound of the ocean and the rustle of palm trees. Camping on Easter Island is about simplicity, intimacy with the landscape, and a deep connection with the island's unique environment.

Campground at Mihinoa: Located on the southwestern coast of Easter Island, Campground at Mihinoa offers an ideal base for exploring the island. This campsite is situated close to the capital, Hanga Roa, providing easy access to the town's amenities while still offering a peaceful retreat. The campground features both tents and small cabins, making it a versatile choice for various travelers. Prices range from $10 to $20 per night, depending on the accommodation type. Amenities include shared kitchen facilities, clean bathrooms with hot showers, and a communal area where guests can socialize. The proximity to the coastline allows for breathtaking sunsets, and the staff can arrange tours and activities, including horseback riding and diving. For those looking to book in advance, the official website provides an easy-to-use reservation system. (https://www.campingmihinoa.com).

Tipanie Moana Camp: Located near the center of Hanga Roa, Tipanie Moana Camp offers a blend of comfort and rustic charm. This campsite is favored by those who seek a more relaxed camping experience without venturing too far from town. The lush greenery surrounding the site provides shade and a serene atmosphere. Accommodation options include private tents and basic cabins, with prices starting at around $15 per night. Guests can enjoy facilities such as shared kitchens, barbecue areas, and Wi-Fi access. What sets Tipanie Moana Camp apart is its commitment to sustainability, with recycling initiatives and solar-powered lighting. The staff is known for their warm hospitality, offering guided tours to explore the island's hidden gems. Meals can be arranged upon request, featuring local delicacies prepared fresh from the island's produce. (https://www.tipaniemoana.com).

Mana Nui Camping: Mana Nui Camping, located just a short walk from the bustling streets of Hanga Roa, provides a more secluded camping experience. The campsite is surrounded by tropical gardens, creating a tranquil escape for nature lovers. Prices for tent spaces begin at $12 per night, with options to rent tents and sleeping gear on-site. The campsite features well-maintained bathrooms, a communal kitchen, and a lounge area where travelers can relax after a day of exploring. Mana Nui Camping is particularly popular among solo travelers and backpackers due to its friendly community atmosphere. The owners often host cultural events, including traditional Rapa Nui music and dance performances, adding an authentic touch to your stay. The nearby coastline is perfect for early morning walks, and the staff can assist with renting bicycles or scooters for a more in-depth exploration of the island. (https://www.manuicamping.com).

Vaiama Camping: Located on the outskirts of Hanga Roa, Vaiama Camping offers a peaceful retreat away from the more crowded tourist areas. This family-run campsite is known for its welcoming atmosphere and personalized service. Accommodation options include tents and small wooden cabins, with prices starting at $18 per night. Vaiama Camping provides all the necessary amenities, including clean restrooms, a shared kitchen, and barbecue facilities.

What makes this campsite unique is its focus on cultural exchange; the owners frequently invite guests to participate in traditional Rapa Nui cooking classes and storytelling sessions. The surrounding landscape is lush and green, offering ample opportunities for nature walks and bird watching. With its emphasis on community and culture, Vaiama Camping provides a rich, immersive experience that goes beyond just a place to sleep. (https://www.vaiamacamping.com).

Camping y Hostal Tipanie Moana: For those who wish to combine the experience of camping with the comfort of a hostel, Camping y Hostal Tipanie Moana offers the best of both worlds. Located near the town center, this hybrid accommodation option provides tents as well as hostel-style rooms. Prices for camping start at $14 per night, while hostel rooms are available at slightly higher rates. Guests have access to shared bathrooms, a fully-equipped kitchen, and a spacious dining area. The on-site restaurant serves breakfast and dinner, with meal prices ranging from $5 to $15. The staff at Camping y Hostal Tipanie Moana are experts in local culture and can arrange various tours, including visits to archaeological sites and traditional dance shows. The blend of camping and hostel facilities makes it an excellent choice for travelers seeking flexibility and comfort. (https://www.tipaniemoanahostel.com).

2.5 Boutique Hotels

These intimate accommodations provide an oasis of comfort and sophistication while allowing guests to experience the island's unique atmosphere. Boutique hotels on Easter Island stand out for their personalized service, exquisite design, and thoughtful amenities that cater to the discerning traveler seeking a memorable stay.

Hotel Hare Uta: Tucked away in the lush landscapes of Rapa Nui, Hotel Hare Uta is a boutique haven offering luxury with a touch of island authenticity. Located just a short drive from Hanga Roa, this hotel is surrounded by gardens that reflect the island's natural beauty. The architecture of Hotel Hare Uta is inspired by traditional Rapa Nui homes, blending local craftsmanship with modern comforts. Rooms start at approximately $300 per night, offering spacious interiors with private terraces that overlook the serene gardens. Amenities include an outdoor pool, a spa offering traditional Polynesian treatments, and a gourmet restaurant that serves dishes crafted from locally-sourced ingredients. The hotel also offers tailored excursions, such as guided tours to the island's archaeological sites and stargazing experiences under the pristine night sky. For those looking to immerse themselves in the island's culture and history, Hotel Hare Uta provides an ideal retreat. (https://www.hareuta.com).

Nayara Hangaroa: Nayara Hangaroa stands as one of Easter Island's premier boutique hotels, offering a blend of eco-conscious design and luxurious accommodations. Situated along the coast near Hanga Roa, the hotel offers panoramic ocean views from every room. The architecture of Nayara Hangaroa reflects the island's volcanic origins, with organic shapes and natural materials used throughout the property. Rooms are priced around $450 per night and come equipped with modern amenities such as air conditioning, free Wi-Fi, and rain showers. The hotel features a wellness center with a range of spa services, an infinity pool overlooking the ocean, and an on-site restaurant that specializes in seafood and Polynesian cuisine. Guests can enjoy a variety of activities, including yoga sessions, cultural workshops, and private tours of the moai statues. Nayara Hangaroa is perfect for travelers who seek an eco-luxury experience on this remote island. (https://www.nayarahangaroa.com).

Hotel Altiplanico Rapa Nui: Perched on a hillside with sweeping views of the Pacific Ocean, Hotel Altiplanico Rapa Nui offers a tranquil escape that harmonizes with the natural surroundings. Located just outside of Hanga Roa, this boutique hotel is designed in the style of a traditional Rapa Nui village, with individual bungalows spread across the lush landscape. The bungalows are constructed using local materials, blending seamlessly with the environment. Room rates start at around $250 per night and include breakfast. The hotel's amenities include an outdoor pool, a restaurant serving fusion cuisine with an emphasis on local ingredients, and a lounge where guests can unwind with a book or enjoy the sunset. Hotel Altiplanico Rapa Nui is known for its peaceful ambiance and is ideal for travelers who wish to disconnect from the hustle and bustle of modern life while still enjoying the comforts of a boutique hotel. (https://www.altiplanico.com).

Taha Tai Hotel: Taha Tai Hotel offers a cozy, boutique experience in the heart of Hanga Roa. This charming hotel is located just a stone's throw from the beach, providing guests with easy access to the ocean and the town's vibrant center. Rooms at Taha Tai Hotel are priced at approximately $200 per night and feature modern amenities such as air conditioning, flat-screen TVs, and private balconies with ocean or garden views. The hotel's facilities include an outdoor swimming pool, a bar serving refreshing cocktails, and a restaurant that offers a diverse menu of local and international dishes. The friendly staff can arrange island tours, cultural shows, and scuba diving excursions. Taha Tai Hotel is perfect for travelers seeking a blend of convenience and comfort, with the added benefit of being close to Hanga Roa's restaurants, shops, and attractions. (https://www.tahatai.com).

O'tai Hotel: O'tai Hotel is one of the oldest boutique hotels on Easter Island, offering a mix of tradition and modernity. Located in the center of Hanga Roa, this family-run hotel has been welcoming guests for decades, providing a warm and authentic experience. The hotel is set within a beautiful garden, where guests can relax and enjoy the tranquility of the island. Rooms are available starting at $180 per night, featuring simple yet comfortable furnishings, with private terraces overlooking the gardens. O'tai Hotel offers a variety of services, including free breakfast, a swimming pool, and a restaurant that serves traditional Rapa Nui dishes. The hotel's staff are known for their hospitality and are happy to organize cultural activities such as dance performances and historical tours. For those looking to stay in a place that combines the convenience of being in the town center with a genuine island experience, O'tai Hotel is an excellent choice. (https://www.otaihotel.com).

2.6 Unique Stays: Eco-Lodges and Island Bungalows

Easter Island also offers unique accommodation options that reflect its rich cultural heritage and natural beauty. Among these are eco-lodges and island bungalows, which provide a perfect blend of comfort, sustainability, and authenticity. Staying in these unique accommodations allows visitors to connect more deeply with the island's environment and culture, making for a truly unforgettable experience.

Eco Lodge Rapa Nui: Located on the outskirts of Hanga Roa, Eco Lodge Rapa Nui offers an intimate and environmentally-conscious retreat. This eco-lodge is designed to harmonize with the island's natural surroundings, using sustainable materials and practices to minimize its environmental footprint. The lodge features charming bungalows built from local materials, each offering privacy and comfort. Prices start at around $220 per night, including breakfast. The bungalows are equipped with solar-powered electricity, rainwater showers, and natural ventilation, ensuring a comfortable stay with minimal environmental impact. The lodge's restaurant serves organic meals made from locally-sourced ingredients, and guests can enjoy activities such as guided eco-tours, hiking, and birdwatching. Eco Lodge Rapa Nui is ideal for travelers who wish to experience the island's beauty in an eco-friendly and responsible way. (https://www.ecolodgerapanui.com).

Hanga Roa Eco Village & Spa: Hanga Roa Eco Village & Spa is a luxurious yet sustainable accommodation option located just a short distance from the town center. The eco-village is set within lush gardens and offers a range of bungalows that combine modern comforts with eco-friendly practices. Rooms start at approximately $350 per night and feature spacious interiors with private terraces, solar-powered lighting, and rainwater collection systems. The on-site spa offers a variety of treatments using natural and locally-sourced ingredients, while the restaurant serves gourmet dishes with a focus on fresh, organic produce. The hotel also offers a range of activities, including yoga classes, cultural workshops, and excursions to explore the island's natural and historical sites. Hanga Roa Eco Village & Spa provides an upscale, sustainable stay that allows guests to indulge in luxury while remaining mindful of the environment. (https://www.hangaroaecovillage.com).

Hare Noi Rapa Nui: Hare Noi Rapa Nui is an exclusive boutique eco-lodge that offers a secluded and luxurious stay on Easter Island. Situated on a hillside with stunning views of the Pacific Ocean, this eco-lodge is designed to blend seamlessly with the natural landscape. The accommodations consist of private bungalows, each featuring modern amenities such as air conditioning, Wi-Fi, and king-sized beds, with prices starting at $400 per night. The lodge places a strong emphasis on sustainability, using solar energy, locally-sourced materials, and organic waste management. The on-site restaurant serves a farm-to-table menu, and guests can participate in activities such as guided hiking tours, traditional Rapa Nui cooking classes, and cultural performances. Hare Noi Rapa Nui is perfect for travelers who seek an intimate, eco-friendly retreat with a focus on luxury and privacy. (https://www.harenoirapanui.com).

Cabanas Anakena: For a more rustic and authentic experience, Cabanas Anakena offers island bungalows that provide a direct connection to Easter Island's cultural heritage. Located near the famous Anakena Beach, these bungalows are built in the traditional Rapa Nui style, with thatched roofs and wooden interiors. Prices for these unique accommodations start at around $150 per night. Each bungalow is equipped with basic amenities, including a kitchenette, a private bathroom, and a terrace with ocean views. Cabanas Anakena is ideal for travelers who wish to immerse themselves in the island's history and natural beauty, with the beach and moai statues just a short walk away. The owners offer personalized services, including guided tours of archaeological sites and cultural experiences, such as traditional dance and storytelling. (https://www.cabanasanakena.com).

Vai Hina Bungalows: Vai Hina Bungalows offers a peaceful and secluded stay in the heart of Easter Island's natural landscape. These bungalows are located on a private property surrounded by lush vegetation, providing a serene and tranquil atmosphere. The bungalows are designed with simplicity and comfort in mind, featuring wooden interiors, comfortable beds, and outdoor seating areas. Prices start at around $120 per night. Vai Hina Bungalows is particularly popular among couples and solo travelers looking for a quiet retreat. The owners are known for their warm hospitality, offering home-cooked meals and personalized tours of the island. Guests can enjoy activities such as horseback riding, hiking, and visiting nearby archaeological sites. Vai Hina Bungalows provides an authentic, off-the-beaten-path experience that allows visitors to fully embrace the island's natural beauty. (https://www.vaihinabungalows.com).

CHAPTER 3
TRANSPORTATION

3.1 Getting Around Easter Island

Navigating Easter Island requires an understanding of its layout. The island, roughly triangular in shape, is centered around Hanga Roa, where most services and accommodations are concentrated. From Hanga Roa, roads radiate outwards to the island's major attractions, including the volcanic craters and moai statues. Familiarizing yourself with this layout will help you plan your routes and ensure you don't miss any of the island's stunning landmarks.

Rent a Bicycle or Scooter: For a unique and enjoyable way to explore Easter Island, consider renting a bicycle or scooter. The island's relatively flat terrain and scenic roads make cycling a pleasant experience. Renting a bicycle or scooter allows you to move at your own pace, explore off-the-beaten-path locations, and enjoy the fresh island air. Rental shops, such as Rapa Nui Rent a Bike, are conveniently located near Hanga Roa, offering a range of options to suit your needs.

Consider Renting a Car: Renting a car provides flexibility and convenience, especially if you plan to visit the island's more remote areas. A vehicle allows you to explore at your own pace, from the iconic Ahu Tongariki to the lush Rano Raraku crater. Several rental agencies in Hanga Roa, like Kava Kava Rent a Car, offer various vehicle options. While driving on Easter Island is straightforward, it's important to be mindful of local driving conditions and regulations.

Utilize Local Tours: Joining a local tour can enhance your experience by providing structured visits to the island's major attractions. Many tours, offered by operators based in Hanga Roa, include transportation and guided commentary. This option is ideal for gaining deeper insights into Easter Island's cultural and historical context while benefiting from the expertise of local guides. Tours can cover significant sites such as the moai statues and ancient ceremonial grounds.

Explore on Foot: Walking is a great way to explore Hanga Roa and its immediate surroundings. The town is compact and pedestrian-friendly, allowing for easy access to local shops, restaurants, and nearby attractions. Walking not only offers a more intimate experience of the town but also lets you appreciate the island's unique atmosphere and discover hidden gems that might be missed when using other modes of transportation.

3.2 Public Transportation Options

Understanding these various public transportation options will enhance your ability to navigate Easter Island effectively, allowing you to enjoy its unique beauty and rich heritage with ease.

Public Buses: Public buses on Easter Island offer a convenient and budget-friendly option for getting around. These buses typically run on set routes connecting Hanga Roa, the island's main town, with several of the island's key attractions. The schedule may vary, so it's advisable to check the latest timetables from local sources or your accommodation. Fares for a single journey are generally between $2 to $4, making it an affordable way to explore sites such as Rano Raraku and Anakena Beach. Buses are a practical choice for those looking to visit well-established tourist destinations without the need for a rental vehicle.

Shared Taxis (Colectivos): Shared taxis, locally known as "colectivos," provide a more flexible alternative to public buses. These taxis operate on specific routes but offer the convenience of picking up and dropping off passengers at various points along the way. This option is particularly useful for accessing areas that might not be directly served by the bus network. The cost of a shared taxi ride depends on the distance traveled and the number of passengers. While it might be slightly more expensive than a bus, it offers a more personalized travel experience. Local drivers or your accommodation can provide updated information on current routes and fares.

Local Tours with Transportation: Local tours that include transportation are another excellent way to get around Easter Island. Many tour operators based in Hanga Roa offer packages that cover major attractions such as the moai statues, volcanic craters, and historical sites. These tours often include transportation as part of the package, allowing you to explore the island with the benefit of a knowledgeable guide. Although this option may be more expensive compared to public transportation, it provides the added value of expert commentary and a structured itinerary. This can be particularly beneficial for those looking to gain deeper insights into the island's cultural and historical significance.

Walking: Walking is a viable option for exploring the town of Hanga Roa and its immediate surroundings. The town is compact and pedestrian-friendly, making it easy to explore local shops, restaurants, and nearby attractions on foot. Walking allows you to interact more intimately with the local environment and discover hidden gems that might not be accessible by other forms of transportation. For short distances and local exploration, walking is not only practical but also provides a more immersive experience of Easter Island's vibrant atmosphere.

3.3 Car Rentals and Driving Tips

Renting a car on Easter Island is a highly recommended option for visitors seeking independence and flexibility. The island's compact size and varied terrain make it an ideal place for driving, allowing you to explore at your own pace while accessing remote and lesser-known spots. Here's a detailed look at car rental options and driving considerations for your visit.

Kava Kava Rent a Car: Several reputable car rental agencies operate on Easter Island, each offering a range of vehicles to suit different needs. Kava Kava Rent a Car, located on Avenida Atamu Tekena in Hanga Roa, is a popular choice. They provide a selection of vehicles from compact cars to 4x4s, with prices starting at approximately $40 per day. Their website, (http://kavakavacarrental.com), offers an easy booking process and additional information on available vehicles.

Rapa Nui Rent a Car: Another well-regarded agency is Rapa Nui Rent a Car, situated near the Hanga Roa waterfront. They offer competitive rates and a variety of vehicle options, including SUVs and small cars. Expect prices to start around $35 per day. Their contact details and rental terms can be found on their website, (http://rapanuirentacar.com).

Hanga Roa Rent a Car: For those seeking a more luxurious experience, Hanga Roa Rent a Car provides premium vehicles and exceptional service. Located at the heart of Hanga Roa, their fleet includes higher-end models and off-road vehicles. Prices begin at approximately $60 per day. More details are available on their website, (http://hangaroarentacar.com).

Easter Island Car Rentals: Easter Island Car Rentals also offers a diverse range of vehicles, from economical options to larger SUVs. Their office is conveniently located in Hanga Roa, and their website, (http://easterislandcarrentals.com), provides up-to-date information on rates and vehicle availability.

Moai Car Rentals: Moai Car Rentals is another viable option, known for their friendly service and competitive rates. Located on Atamu Tekena Street, their website, (http://moaicarrentals.com), features comprehensive details on their vehicle lineup and rental policies.

Driving on Easter Island requires some special considerations. The island's roads are generally well-maintained but can be narrow and winding, especially near the volcanic craters. Driving is on the right side of the road, and local traffic regulations should be followed to ensure safety. Many rental agencies offer GPS units or detailed maps to help you navigate the island's attractions.

3.4 Cycling and Walking on Easter Island

For those seeking an immersive way to explore this remote paradise, cycling and walking offer unparalleled experiences. The island's diverse terrain and cultural treasures are best appreciated at a leisurely pace, whether you're pedaling through its scenic routes or hiking to historical sites. This guide delves into the island's most captivating cycling and walking routes, providing detailed insights into navigating Easter Island's natural beauty and historical wonders. Whether you're an avid cyclist or a casual walker, Easter Island promises an unforgettable journey filled with adventure and discovery.

Cycling Routes on Easter Island
Hanga Roa to Anakena Beach: Cycling from Hanga Roa to Anakena Beach is one of the most iconic routes on Easter Island. This 15-kilometer journey offers a flat, scenic ride with occasional gentle inclines. Starting from the island's main town, Hanga Roa, cyclists will traverse through lush landscapes and coastal views, arriving at the stunning Anakena Beach. Along the way, the route passes several significant archaeological sites, including moai statues that are emblematic of the island's rich cultural heritage. This route is accessible for cyclists of various skill levels and provides an excellent introduction to Easter Island's beauty.

Hanga Roa to Rano Raraku: The route from Hanga Roa to Rano Raraku is a must-ride for those interested in the island's history. Covering approximately 12 kilometers, this trail leads to the famous moai quarry where the iconic statues were carved. The route features a combination of gentle slopes and flat stretches, making it manageable for most cyclists. Riders will be rewarded with views of the moai statues scattered around the quarry, offering a direct connection to the island's historical narrative.

Rano Kau to Orongo: For a more challenging cycling experience, the route from Rano Kau to Orongo offers a mix of steep inclines and rugged terrain. This 20-kilometer trail ascends to the Rano Kau crater, providing cyclists with panoramic views of the island. The ride continues to the ceremonial village of Orongo, known for its cultural significance and breathtaking vistas. This route is ideal for experienced cyclists seeking both physical challenges and cultural exploration.

Hanga Roa to Poike Peninsula: Cycling from Hanga Roa to the Poike Peninsula is an 18-kilometer route that takes riders through diverse landscapes, from volcanic craters to verdant areas. The trail features a combination of smooth and rough sections, offering a varied cycling experience. The Poike Peninsula, with its remote and tranquil atmosphere, provides an opportunity for cyclists to escape the crowds and enjoy the island's natural beauty in a more secluded setting.

Hanga Roa to Ahu Tongariki: For a shorter, more relaxed ride, the 10-kilometer route from Hanga Roa to Ahu Tongariki is ideal. This route leads to the island's largest moai platform, showcasing an impressive array of statues. The trail is relatively flat and straightforward, making it suitable for cyclists of all levels. The opportunity to view the iconic moai up close makes this route a popular choice for those interested in the island's cultural landmarks.

Walking Routes on Easter Island
Rano Kau Crater Loop: The Rano Kau Crater Loop is one of the most rewarding walking trails on Easter Island. This 5-kilometer loop circles the island's largest volcanic crater, offering stunning views of the crater lake and the surrounding landscape. The trail is moderately easy, with gentle inclines and flat sections, making it accessible for walkers of various fitness levels. Along the way, walkers can enjoy the serene environment and explore the rich geological features of the crater.

Rano Raraku Quarry Trail: Walking to Rano Raraku, the moai quarry, is a deeply immersive experience. This trail, approximately 4 kilometers long, allows visitors to closely examine the site where the iconic statues were crafted. The walk takes you through the quarry and around the area where numerous moai are still found in various stages of completion. The trail provides insight into the island's ancient stone-carving techniques and offers a profound connection to Easter Island's cultural heritage.

Orongo Ceremonial Village: The walking trail to Orongo, a historic ceremonial village located on the rim of the Rano Kau crater, is a 6-kilometer trek that combines historical exploration with scenic beauty. The trail ascends to the village, offering spectacular views of the crater and the surrounding landscape. The path includes some moderate inclines and rugged terrain but is manageable for most walkers. At Orongo, visitors can explore the ruins of the ceremonial village and learn about the birdman cult that once dominated the island's spiritual practices.

Anakena Beach Coastal Walk: For a leisurely stroll, the coastal walk from Anakena Beach offers a relaxing experience with picturesque views of the ocean and the island's coastline. This 3-kilometer trail is flat and easy to navigate, making it suitable for casual walkers and families. Along the route, visitors can enjoy the beach's golden sands and the iconic moai statues that line the shore, providing a beautiful setting for a peaceful walk.

Hanga Roa to Ahu Akivi: The walk from Hanga Roa to Ahu Akivi, located approximately 8 kilometers away, is a moderately challenging route that offers a chance to explore one of the island's important moai platforms. The trail features a mix of flat sections and gentle slopes, making it accessible for most walkers. At Ahu Akivi, visitors can admire the seven moai statues, which are unique for their alignment towards the ocean. The walk provides both a cultural and scenic experience, showcasing the island's rich heritage and natural beauty.

3.5 Shuttle Services

These shuttle services provide convenient and reliable transportation for visitors, ensuring access to key attractions and seamless travel between various points of interest. Understanding the available shuttle services can greatly enhance your experience, allowing you to explore the island's rich history and stunning landscapes without the stress of navigating on your own.

Rapa Nui Shuttle Services

Rapa Nui Shuttle Services is a well-regarded company offering a range of transportation options for visitors. Located in the heart of Hanga Roa, the main town on Easter Island, Rapa Nui Shuttle Services provides convenient access to various parts of the island. Their contact address is Avenida Pont, Hanga Roa. For more information or to make reservations, visitors can visit their website at www.rapanuishuttle.com. Prices for their services vary depending on the route and duration, but typically start around $30 USD for a one-way trip.

Easter Island Transport

Easter Island Transport is another reliable option for getting around the island. Their office is situated in Hanga Roa, and they offer a range of shuttle services including airport transfers, island tours, and private transportation. Their website, www.easterislandtransport.cl, provides detailed information about their services and booking options. Prices for shuttle services with Easter Island Transport start at approximately $35 USD for local transfers and can vary based on the type of service and distance.

Terevaka Expeditions

Terevaka Expeditions offers both shuttle and tour services, catering to visitors who want to combine transportation with guided exploration. Based in Hanga Roa, their office is located on Calle Pukao. Visitors can visit their website at www.terevakaexpeditions.com. Terevaka Expeditions provides a range of packages, including airport transfers and island tours, with prices starting at around $40 USD for basic shuttle services.

Hanga Roa Shuttle

Hanga Roa Shuttle is known for its punctual and reliable service, making it a popular choice among travelers. Their office is located on Av. Te Pito o Te Henua, Hanga Roa. For more information or to book a service, visitors can check their website at www.hangaroashuttle.cl. Shuttle services with Hanga Roa Shuttle start at about $25 USD, with options for both standard transfers and private shuttles available.

Easter Island Tours & Transfers

Easter Island Tours & Transfers offers a variety of shuttle and tour options designed to enhance the visitor experience. Their office is conveniently located in Hanga Roa on Av. Te Moana. Visit their website at www.easterislandtours.com. They provide competitive pricing for their shuttle services, starting from around $30 USD, with options for both scheduled transfers and customized tours available.

Additional Information for Visitors

When using shuttle services on Easter Island, it is advisable to book in advance, especially during peak travel seasons. Many shuttle services offer customizable packages, including airport pickups, private tours, and transport to specific attractions. It's also beneficial to check the availability of English-speaking drivers or guides if you're not fluent in Spanish. For those looking to explore the island extensively, some companies offer multi-day passes or extended packages that can provide better value and flexibility. Ensuring you have all the necessary contact information and understanding the pricing structure will help you navigate Easter Island smoothly and make the most of your visit.

CHAPTER 4
TOP 10 ATTRACTIONS & HIDDEN GEMS

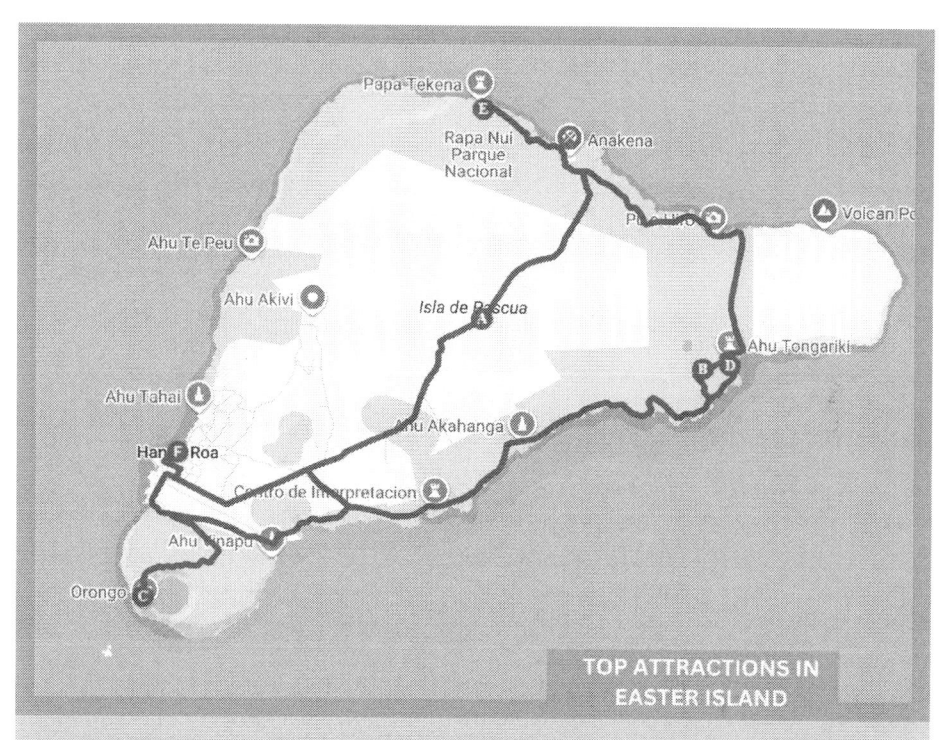

Directions from Easter Island, Chile to Ovahe, Easter Island, Chile

A
Easter Island, Chile

B
Rano Raraku, Easter Island, Chile

E
Rapa Nui National Park, Easter Island, Chile

C
Orongo, Easter Island, Chile

F
Hanga Roa, Easter Island, Chile

D
Ahu Tongariki, Easter Island, Chile

G
Ovahe, Easter Island, Chile

4.1 Moai Statues

Moai statues stand as silent sentinels, guarding the secrets of a civilization long past. Each Moai tells a story of ancestors, power, and belief—and to walk among them is to step into a world where the ancient and the timeless converge. This island beckons the curious traveler to explore its sacred grounds, where every stone, every carving, holds a whisper of the past. Here are five unmissable places to encounter these colossal figures in all their glory.

Ahu Nau Nau
Perched on the beautiful white sands of Anakena Beach, Ahu Nau Nau is a site where history and paradise meet. These Moai statues are some of the best-preserved on the island, thanks to being buried in sand for centuries. The intricate carvings on their backs, depicting ancient tattoos and other sacred symbols, speak of the islanders' reverence for their ancestors. Visiting Ahu Nau Nau not only offers a glimpse into the artistic prowess of the Rapa Nui people but also provides the perfect opportunity to relax on the beach, letting the serene surroundings enhance your sense of wonder.

Ahu Akivi

Unlike most Moai, which face inland, the seven statues at Ahu Akivi gaze out towards the ocean, a rare and haunting sight. These Moai are believed to represent the seven explorers sent by the legendary founder of Rapa Nui, Hotu Matu'a, to find the island. Positioned with astronomical precision, Ahu Akivi also serves as a celestial observatory, aligning with the equinoxes. Visiting this site at dusk, as the sun sets behind the ocean, you'll be struck by a sense of alignment not just of stars and statues, but of the human spirit with the cosmos—a timeless connection that transcends the ages.

Ahu Hanga Te'e

Tucked away on the eastern shore, Ahu Hanga Te'e is one of the lesser-known but equally compelling Moai sites on Easter Island. This site has a melancholic beauty, with toppled Moai lying face down, as if in deep slumber, a stark reminder of the island's turbulent past. The sense of mystery here is palpable—why were these statues overthrown? What stories do they still hold, waiting to be uncovered? Hanga Te'e invites the curious traveler to ponder the rise and fall of civilizations, to feel the weight of history in the presence of these fallen giants.

4.2 Rano Raraku Volcano

This extinct volcano served as the quarry for nearly all of the island's Moai statues, and today, it stands as a testament to the ingenuity and dedication of the Rapa Nui people. To visit Rano Raraku is to step into a world where nature and human ambition collided to create something truly extraordinary. The landscape here is like no other filled with the half-formed, half-forgotten faces of history, waiting to be discovered. Here are five places within this sacred site that you must explore to fully appreciate the wonder of Rano Raraku.

The Quarry: The quarry at Rano Raraku is the very soul of the Moai statues. As you walk along its slopes, you'll find over 400 Moai in various stages of completion, some still attached to the rock, as if the stone was never fully willing to let them go. Each statue here tells a story of creation—of how the Rapa Nui people transformed volcanic rock into representations of their ancestors. The sight of these silent giants, some standing tall, others lying in eternal repose, is both haunting and awe-inspiring. It's a place that speaks to the power of human creativity and the enduring mystery of the Moai.

The Moai of Tukuturi: Among the many Moai at Rano Raraku, one stands out for its distinctiveness—Tukuturi, the kneeling Moai. Unlike the others, this statue has a more human-like appearance, with a beard and bent knees, possibly representing a singer or a priest in a state of spiritual contemplation. Tukuturi's presence adds a layer of intrigue to the site, offering a glimpse into the cultural and spiritual life of the Rapa Nui people. Standing before Tukuturi, you can't help but wonder about the rituals and ceremonies that took place here, and the deep connection the islanders had with their spiritual world.

The Moai on the Southern Slopes: The southern slopes of Rano Raraku are home to a parade of Moai statues, some partially buried, others proudly standing, their faces turned towards the sky. This area is less visited than the main quarry, offering a more intimate and contemplative experience. Here, the statues seem to blend into the landscape, becoming one with the earth from which they were born. The tranquility of this place, combined with the solemn expressions of the Moai, creates a powerful atmosphere—one that invites quiet reflection and a deep appreciation for the island's history and natural beauty.

The Moai Inside the Crater: Rano Raraku's crater is a world unto itself, a hidden sanctuary where nature and history coexist in perfect harmony. The crater's lake, surrounded by lush vegetation, is home to several Moai that seem to guard this secluded paradise. The contrast between the green landscape and the stone figures creates a striking visual, one that feels almost otherworldly. Exploring the crater is like stepping into a forgotten chapter of Easter Island's story, where the Moai stand not as monuments to the past, but as guardians of a living, breathing ecosystem that has thrived for centuries.

The Moai of Piro Piro: Piro Piro, located on the eastern side of Rano Raraku, is home to some of the tallest Moai on the island. These towering figures, carved from the volcanic rock, stand as silent sentinels overlooking the ocean. The sheer size and scale of these Moai are staggering, and as you stand beneath them, you can't help but feel a sense of awe at the incredible skill and determination it took to create them. The view from Piro Piro is breathtaking, offering a panoramic vista of the island's rugged coastline—a reminder of the indomitable spirit of the Rapa Nui people and their enduring connection to the land.

4.3 Anakena Beach

Imagine a pristine beach where history meets paradise, this is Anakena, Easter Island's most famous stretch of sand. Known for its breathtaking beauty and historical significance, Anakena Beach offers visitors a unique blend of relaxation and cultural immersion. The warm waters of the Pacific Ocean gently lap against the shore, while the towering Moai statues stand guard, their gazes fixed on the horizon. This is a place where legends were born, where the first Polynesian settlers are said to have landed, and where you can experience the timeless allure of Easter Island in a setting that feels almost otherworldly. Here are must-see places at Anakena Beach that will leave you spellbound.

Ahu Nau Nau: Ahu Nau Nau, the main Moai platform at Anakena, is a site that embodies the perfect fusion of history and natural beauty. These seven Moai statues, some of the best-preserved on the island, stand proudly on the edge of the beach, their intricate carvings a testament to the skill of the ancient Rapa Nui carvers. The statues' backs are adorned with detailed designs, including representations of the traditional loincloth, or "hami," worn by the islanders. As you stand before Ahu Nau Nau, with the crystal-clear waters of Anakena lapping at your feet, you can't help but feel a deep connection to the island's past—a past that lives on in the very stones that have stood here for centuries.

Ahu Ature Huki: A short walk from Ahu Nau Nau, you'll find Ahu Ature Huki, a single Moai statue that holds a special place in the history of Easter Island. This was the first Moai to be re-erected by the islanders in 1956, under the direction of the legendary explorer Thor Heyerdahl. The statue, which had lain toppled for centuries, was raised using traditional methods, providing invaluable insights into the techniques used by the Rapa Nui people. A visit to Ahu Ature Huki is not just an opportunity to see a Moai, but to witness a moment in history—one that marked the beginning of the island's cultural revival.

The White Sands of Anakena: Anakena Beach is more than just a historical site; it's also one of the most beautiful beaches in the world. The soft, white sand contrasts sharply with the rugged volcanic landscape of the rest of the island, creating a tropical oasis that feels almost surreal. The turquoise waters are perfect for swimming, offering a refreshing escape from the island's intense sun. Palm trees sway gently in the breeze, and the sound of waves breaking on the shore creates a soothing soundtrack to your visit. Whether you're here to relax, swim, or simply take in the stunning scenery, Anakena Beach offers a slice of paradise that's hard to find anywhere else.

The Legends of Hotu Matu'a: Anakena is not just a place of beauty; it's also steeped in legend. According to tradition, this beach is where the first Polynesian settlers, led by the legendary king Hotu Matu'a, landed after their long voyage from Hiva, the mythical homeland. As you walk along the shore, you can almost imagine the canoes arriving, the first steps of a new civilization being taken on these sands. The spirit of discovery and adventure that brought those early settlers to Easter Island is still palpable here, making Anakena a place where history and legend are intertwined, waiting for you to uncover their secrets.

The Easter Island Festival: If you're lucky enough to visit Anakena during the Tapati Rapa Nui festival, you'll experience the beach in a whole new light. This annual event, held in February, is a vibrant celebration of Rapa Nui culture, featuring traditional music, dance, and competitions. Anakena becomes the heart of the festivities, with locals and visitors alike gathering to honor the island's heritage. The beach comes alive with the sounds of drums and chants, the sight of colorful costumes, and the energy of the performances. It's a celebration that brings the past into the present, allowing you to immerse yourself in the rich cultural tapestry of Easter Island.

4.4 Orongo Birdman Cult Site

Perched on the edge of a volcanic crater, high above the Pacific Ocean, lies Orongo, a site steeped in mystery and cultural significance. This ancient ceremonial village was once the center of the Birdman cult, a unique aspect of Rapa Nui's history that continues to intrigue and fascinate visitors. Here, the cliffs drop dramatically into the sea, and the island's sacred islets—Motu Nui, Motu Iti, and Motu Kao Kao—stand as silent witnesses to the rituals that once took place. Orongo is a place where you can feel the presence of the past, where the landscape and the legends of the Birdman merge into a powerful narrative. Here are must-see places at Orongo that will take you on a journey through the spiritual heart of Easter Island.

The Ceremonial Village: The village of Orongo is unlike any other on Easter Island. This ceremonial site, perched on the rim of the Rano Kau crater, consists of more than fifty stone houses, each built in the unique elliptical style of the islanders. These low, narrow structures were used by the Birdman competitors and priests during the annual Tangata Manu competition—a grueling test of endurance and bravery. Walking through Orongo, you can almost hear the echoes of the past, feel the tension in the air as competitors prepared for their perilous descent to the sea. The village offers a rare glimpse into the spiritual and social life of the Rapa Nui people, making it an essential stop on your journey through Easter Island.

The Birdman Petroglyphs: Orongo is home to some of the most important petroglyphs on Easter Island, with hundreds of carvings depicting the Birdman (Tangata Manu), sacred birds, and other symbols of the island's rich mythology. These petroglyphs, etched into the basalt rock, tell the story of the Birdman cult—a unique religious and political system that dominated the island for centuries. The most famous of these carvings is the Birdman figure, with its distinctive human body and bird-like head, representing the spiritual and physical connection between humans and the gods. As you study these ancient carvings, you'll be drawn into the world of the Rapa Nui, where art and belief were inextricably linked, and where the Birdman was both a symbol of power and a bridge to the divine.

The View of Motu Nui: From Orongo, the view of Motu Nui, the largest of the three sacred islets, is nothing short of breathtaking. This rocky outcrop, rising from the ocean like a sentinel, was the focal point of the Birdman competition. Competitors would swim to Motu Nui to retrieve the first egg of the sooty tern, a daring feat that required both physical strength and spiritual favor. Standing at the edge of the cliff, looking out over the vast expanse of the ocean, you can almost feel the presence of those who risked their lives in the name of tradition. The view of Motu Nui is a reminder of the island's deep connection to the sea, and the powerful rituals that once defined life on Easter Island.

The Crater of Rano Kau: Orongo is not only a place of cultural significance but also one of extraordinary natural beauty. The Rano Kau crater, on whose rim Orongo sits, is a stunning geological wonder. The crater is nearly a mile in diameter, and its interior is filled with a freshwater lake, dotted with floating islands of reeds. The contrast between the lush greenery of the crater and the stark cliffs of Orongo creates a landscape of incredible beauty. Exploring the crater's edge, you'll be captivated by the panoramic views of the island and the ocean beyond. Rano Kau is a reminder of the powerful forces of nature that have shaped Easter Island, and the harmonious relationship between the islanders and their environment.

The Reconstructed Ceremonial Houses: In recent years, several of the stone houses at Orongo have been carefully reconstructed, offering visitors a chance to step back in time and experience the site as it once was. These houses, with their low entrances and stone slab roofs, provide a tangible connection to the past, allowing you to imagine what life was like for the Birdman competitors and the priests who oversaw the rituals. The reconstruction has been done with great respect for the original structures, preserving the integrity of the site while making it more accessible to visitors. Walking through these houses, you'll gain a deeper understanding of the cultural and spiritual significance of Orongo, and the enduring legacy of the Birdman cult.

4.5 Ahu Tongariki

Perched on the southeastern coast of Easter Island, Ahu Tongariki stands as a grand testament to the island's storied past and rich cultural heritage. This awe-inspiring archaeological site is home to the largest collection of Moai statues on the island, each one silently narrating the epic saga of the Rapa Nui people. As you approach Ahu Tongariki, the sheer scale and grandeur of the site will leave you breathless, compelling you to delve deeper into its mysteries and marvels. Here, amidst the towering statues and dramatic landscapes, you will find a sense of wonder and reverence that transcends time. A visit to Ahu Tongariki is not just a journey through history, but a profound encounter with the spirit of Easter Island.

The Iconic Moai Statues: The highlight of Ahu Tongariki is undoubtedly its impressive lineup of 15 Moai statues, the largest concentration on the island. Standing majestically on their ceremonial platform, these statues represent the ancestors of the Rapa Nui people, their gaze set solemnly toward the sea. Each Moai is a masterpiece of ancient artistry, with detailed carvings and expressive faces that capture the essence of their creators' spiritual beliefs. As you stand among these colossal figures, you can feel the weight of history pressing in, as if the spirits of the past are reaching out to connect with the present. The sheer scale of the Moai, combined with their mysterious presence, creates an unforgettable experience that will leave you in awe of the island's cultural legacy.

The Restoration Story: Ahu Tongariki's Moai statues were not always in such pristine condition. In the 1960s, the site was ravaged by a devastating tsunami, toppling the Moai and scattering their fragments across the beach. The subsequent restoration effort, led by a dedicated team of archaeologists and local Rapa Nui, is a remarkable story of revival and resilience. As you explore the site, you can appreciate the meticulous work that went into restoring the Moai to their former glory, a testament to the commitment of preserving the island's heritage. This narrative of restoration adds an extra layer of depth to your visit, offering insight into the challenges and triumphs of safeguarding Easter Island's cultural treasures.

The Sunrise Experience: For a truly magical experience, visit Ahu Tongariki at sunrise. As the first rays of sunlight kiss the Moai statues, a warm, golden light bathes the scene, creating a breathtaking visual spectacle. The tranquil morning atmosphere, combined with the dramatic interplay of light and shadow on the Moai, offers a serene and contemplative start to the day. The sunrise at Ahu Tongariki is more than just a beautiful sight; it is a moment of connection with the island's spiritual essence, as if the ancient guardians are awakening to greet the new day. Arriving early allows you to witness this profound moment in solitude, making it a truly memorable and personal experience.

The Scenic Backdrop: Ahu Tongariki is not only a cultural treasure but also a visual masterpiece set against a stunning natural backdrop. The site overlooks the vast Pacific Ocean, with dramatic cliffs and rolling hills framing the view. The contrast between the rugged coastline and the serene Moai statues creates a striking landscape that is both majestic and serene. As you explore the site, take a moment to appreciate the interplay between human artistry and natural beauty, where the ancient statues seem to harmonize with their surroundings. The setting of Ahu Tongariki enhances the experience, making it a place where history and nature come together in perfect harmony.

The Spiritual Connection: Visiting Ahu Tongariki offers more than just a glimpse into the past; it provides a profound opportunity for personal reflection and spiritual connection. The presence of the Moai, with their solemn expressions and commanding stature, invites you to contemplate the deeper meanings behind their creation. As you walk among these ancient guardians, you may find yourself reflecting on the values and beliefs of the Rapa Nui people, as well as your own sense of place in the world. The site has a serene and contemplative atmosphere that encourages introspection, making it a place where you can connect with the spiritual essence of Easter Island and experience a sense of peace and reverence.

4.6 Easter Island National Park

At the heart of this enigmatic island lies Easter Island National Park, a UNESCO World Heritage Site that holds the island's most treasured secrets. This park is not just a place to visit; it is a journey into the past, where each step brings you closer to understanding the rich heritage and untamed landscapes of this remote paradise. Here, the towering Moai statues stand as silent sentinels, watching over the island's windswept plains and rugged coastlines. Let your curiosity lead you through these sacred grounds, where every stone has a story to tell, and every vista invites you to reflect on the mysteries of a civilization long gone.

Ahu Akivi: Unlike most Moai, which face inland, the seven statues at Ahu Akivi gaze out towards the ocean. According to legend, these Moai represent the seven explorers sent by the island's first king to find this remote paradise. Standing on a platform in the midst of open grassland, these statues are aligned with the equinox, their eyes fixed on the horizon as if waiting for something—or someone to arrive. Ahu Akivi is a place of reflection, where the past and present seem to merge in the silence of the landscape. The site offers a different perspective on the Moai, one that emphasizes the island's deep connection to the sea and the stars.

Ahu Tahai: Ahu Tahai is one of the oldest ceremonial platforms on Easter Island, and it is here that you can witness one of the most spectacular sunsets on the island. As the sun dips below the horizon, the Moai at Ahu Tahai are bathed in a golden light, their stoic expressions softened by the fading day. This site, which includes three restored platforms, is a place where time seems to stand still, allowing you to connect with the ancient spirits that once guided the Rapa Nui people. The quiet beauty of Ahu Tahai, combined with the setting sun, creates a moment of serenity that will stay with you long after you leave the island.

4.7 Caves of Easter Island

Beneath the windswept plains and rugged coastlines of Easter Island lies a hidden world that few visitors ever explore the caves of Easter Island. These subterranean wonders are not just natural formations; they are living archives of the island's history, used by the Rapa Nui people for shelter, refuge, and sacred ceremonies. Each cave has its own story, etched into the walls by the passage of time and the hands of those who sought solace within. Exploring these caves is like stepping into another realm, where the air is thick with mystery, and the darkness hides secrets that have remained undisturbed for centuries. Venture into this underworld, and you will discover a side of Easter Island that is both haunting and mesmerizing, a place where the island's ancient past is preserved in stone and shadow.

Ana Te Pahu: Ana Te Pahu is the largest cave on Easter Island and is often referred to as the Cave of Bananas due to the lush vegetation that thrives near its entrance. This cave was once a vital source of water and shelter for the Rapa Nui people, and its spacious chambers reveal evidence of ancient habitation. As you descend into the cave, the temperature drops, and the air becomes cooler, offering a welcome respite from the island's tropical heat. The cave's walls, carved by volcanic forces, are adorned with natural formations that resemble frozen waves, creating an otherworldly atmosphere. Exploring Ana Te Pahu, you can almost hear the echoes of the past, the whispers of those who once sought refuge in its depths.

Ana Kakenga: Ana Kakenga is known as the Cave of Two Windows, a fitting name for this narrow tunnel that leads to two openings overlooking the Pacific Ocean. The journey to reach these windows is both exhilarating and eerie, as the cave's dark passage twists and turns before revealing the breathtaking view of the crashing waves below. This cave was likely used as a hiding place during times of conflict, its concealed entrance offering protection from invaders. Standing at the edge of the openings, with the wind whipping through your hair and the sea roaring below, you feel a deep connection to the island's tumultuous history and the resilience of its people.

Ana Kai Tangata: Ana Kai Tangata, translated as the Cave of Cannibals, is a place steeped in legend and dark mystery. The name alone is enough to send shivers down your spine, but the cave's true allure lies in the ancient paintings that adorn its walls. These vibrant petroglyphs depict birds, boats, and human figures, offering a glimpse into the island's cultural and spiritual practices. The cave's location, overlooking the ocean, adds to its mystique, as the sound of the waves echoes through the chambers, amplifying the sense of isolation and foreboding. Whether the cave's name is a reference to actual cannibalistic practices or simply a symbolic warning, Ana Kai Tangata is a place that stirs the imagination and invites you to ponder the island's enigmatic past.

Ana Te Pora: Ana Te Pora is a lesser-known cave, often overlooked by visitors in favor of more famous sites. However, those who venture into this hidden sanctuary are rewarded with a sense of peace and solitude that is hard to find elsewhere on the island. The cave's entrance is concealed by dense vegetation, creating a natural barrier that adds to its secretive allure. Inside, the cave opens into a spacious chamber, its walls smooth and cool to the touch. This cave was likely used for spiritual ceremonies or as a place of retreat, where the Rapa Nui people could escape the pressures of daily life. The quiet stillness of Ana Te Pora invites you to reflect on the deeper connections between the island's natural and spiritual worlds.

Ana Kiri: Ana Kiri is one of the most spiritually significant caves on Easter Island, believed to be a resting place for the island's ancestors. The cave's entrance is marked by a stone platform, where offerings were once made to honor the spirits of the departed. Inside, the cave is dark and narrow, with only a faint light filtering through small openings in the rock. The atmosphere is thick with reverence, as if the spirits of the past still linger in the shadows. Visiting Ana Kiri is a humbling experience, one that reminds you of the deep respect the Rapa Nui people had for their ancestors and the land they called home.

4.8 Easter Island Museum

The Easter Island Museum, also known as the Museo Antropológico Padre Sebastián Englert, is more than just a repository of artifacts; it is a gateway to the island's soul. In the heart of Hanga Roa, this museum is a treasure trove of history, culture, and mystery, where every exhibit tells a story of the Rapa Nui people and their incredible journey across the ages. As you step into the museum, you are not merely entering a building; you are embarking on a voyage through time, guided by the relics and memories of a civilization that defied the odds to create a legacy that endures to this day. The Easter Island Museum is a place of learning and wonder, where the island's past comes to life in vivid detail, inviting you to explore its many layers of meaning.

The Moai Collection: The museum's Moai collection is perhaps its most famous exhibit, offering a rare opportunity to see these iconic statues up close and in a controlled environment. Unlike the Moai scattered across the island, those in the museum have been meticulously preserved, allowing you to appreciate the craftsmanship and artistry that went into their creation. Each statue has its own unique features, from the expressions on their faces to the intricate carvings that adorn their bodies. As you stand before these ancient guardians, you can almost feel the presence of the Rapa Nui people who carved them, their hopes, fears, and beliefs etched into every line. The Moai collection is a powerful reminder of the island's spiritual and cultural heritage, a connection that transcends time.

The Rongorongo Tablets: One of the most intriguing exhibits in the Easter Island Museum is the collection of Rongorongo tablets, wooden artifacts inscribed with a mysterious script that has yet to be fully deciphered. These tablets are believed to contain the written records of the Rapa Nui people, offering a tantalizing glimpse into their thoughts, stories, and rituals. The script, with its flowing lines and complex symbols, is unlike any other writing system in the world, adding to the enigma of Easter Island. Scholars and linguists have long debated the meaning of Rongorongo, but its secrets remain elusive. As you examine these tablets, you are drawn into the mystery, compelled to imagine the knowledge and wisdom they may hold.

The Cultural Artifacts: The museum's collection of cultural artifacts provides a window into the daily life of the Rapa Nui people, from their tools and clothing to their art and religious objects. These items, often simple in design, reveal the resourcefulness and creativity of a people who thrived in isolation. The tools, crafted from stone and bone, show how the Rapa Nui adapted to their environment, while the woven clothing and ornaments highlight their connection to nature. The religious artifacts, including ceremonial statues and ritual objects, offer insight into the island's spiritual practices, where every aspect of life was intertwined with the sacred. Walking through this exhibit, you gain a deeper understanding of the Rapa Nui people and the rich cultural tapestry they created.

The Archaeological Discoveries: The Easter Island Museum also houses a collection of archaeological finds that shed light on the island's ancient history. These discoveries, ranging from ancient tools and pottery to the remains of ancient settlements, provide crucial evidence of the island's long and complex history. One of the most fascinating exhibits is the display of ancient burial sites, where the remains of the island's earliest inhabitants are preserved. These burial sites, with their carefully arranged bones and grave goods, offer a poignant reminder of the island's past and the people who once called it home. The archaeological discoveries in the museum are a testament to the island's rich history, a history that continues to be uncovered with each new find.

The Interactive Exhibits: The Easter Island Museum is not just about looking at artifacts; it is also about engaging with history in a meaningful way. The museum offers a range of interactive exhibits that allow visitors to immerse themselves in the world of the Rapa Nui people. From virtual tours of ancient sites to hands-on activities that teach traditional crafts, these exhibits provide a deeper connection to the island's culture and history. One of the highlights is the 3D reconstruction of a Moai carving, where you can see how these massive statues were created and transported across the island. These interactive exhibits make the museum a dynamic and engaging experience, where history comes to life in new and exciting ways.

4.9 Hanga Roa Town

Hanga Roa, the capital and only town on Easter Island, is the vibrant heart of this remote paradise. It is here that the island's past and present meet, where ancient traditions are kept alive amidst the hustle and bustle of modern life. Hanga Roa is not just a place to pass through; it is a destination in itself, full of charm, culture, and hidden treasures. As you wander through its streets, you will find yourself drawn to its warm and welcoming atmosphere, where every corner offers something new to discover. From the lively markets to the tranquil shores, Hanga Roa is a place that invites you to slow down, take in the sights and sounds, and connect with the island's unique way of life.

The Hanga Roa Market: The Hanga Roa Market is the perfect place to experience the local culture of Easter Island. This bustling market is a feast for the senses, with stalls selling everything from fresh produce and seafood to handmade crafts and souvenirs. The market is a hub of activity, where locals and visitors alike come to shop, socialize, and enjoy the vibrant atmosphere. The aromas of grilled fish and tropical fruits fill the air, tempting you to sample the island's delicious cuisine. The market is also a great place to find unique gifts and mementos, from intricately carved wooden statues to colorful textiles. A visit to the Hanga Roa Market is a must for anyone looking to immerse themselves in the culture and daily life of Easter Island.

The Church of Holy Cross: The Church of Holy Cross, known locally as La Iglesia de la Santa Cruz, is a beautiful and serene place of worship in the heart of Hanga Roa. This small church, with its simple yet elegant architecture, is a symbol of the island's deep spiritual roots. The interior is adorned with traditional Rapa Nui artwork, including statues and carvings that blend Christian and indigenous motifs. Attending a service here is a moving experience, as the sound of hymns sung in the Rapa Nui language fills the air, creating a sense of unity and peace. The church is also a place of reflection, where you can sit quietly and contemplate the island's rich spiritual heritage.

The Tahai Ceremonial Complex: Just a short walk from the center of Hanga Roa lies the Tahai Ceremonial Complex, one of the most important archaeological sites on the island. This site is home to several restored Ahu (ceremonial platforms) and Moai statues, including the only Moai with restored eyes. The location, overlooking the ocean, is breathtaking, especially at sunset when the statues are silhouetted against the colorful sky. The Tahai Complex offers a glimpse into the island's ancient past, where the Moai once served as guardians of the Rapa Nui people. It is a place of quiet contemplation, where the beauty of the landscape and the history of the island come together in perfect harmony.

The Sebastian Englert Anthropological Museum: The Sebastian Englert Anthropological Museum is a must-visit for anyone interested in the history and culture of Easter Island. Located on the outskirts of Hanga Roa, this museum offers a comprehensive overview of the island's history, from its earliest settlers to the present day. The museum's exhibits include ancient artifacts, traditional clothing, and detailed models of the island's famous Moai statues. One of the highlights is the collection of Rongorongo tablets, which are inscribed with the mysterious script that has yet to be fully deciphered. The museum provides valuable context for understanding the island's unique culture and is a great starting point for anyone looking to explore Easter Island in depth.

The Hanga Roa Pier: The Hanga Roa Pier is the starting point for many of the island's water-based activities, from snorkeling and diving to boat tours and fishing trips. The clear waters around the pier are teeming with marine life, making it a popular spot for snorkeling and diving enthusiasts. The pier is also a great place to watch the fishermen bring in their catch, a tradition that has been passed down through generations. For those looking to explore the island's coastline, boat tours offer a unique perspective on the island's natural beauty, with stops at remote beaches and hidden coves. The Hanga Roa Pier is a place of excitement and adventure, where the possibilities for exploration are endless.

4.10 Ovahe Beach

Tucked away on the northeastern coast of Easter Island lies Ovahe Beach, a hidden gem that offers a serene escape from the island's more well-known attractions. Unlike the bustling shores of Anakena, Ovahe Beach is a place of solitude and natural beauty, where the turquoise waters gently lap against the pinkish sands, and the rugged cliffs provide a dramatic backdrop. This secluded beach is a haven for those seeking peace and tranquility, a place where you can disconnect from the outside world and immerse yourself in the island's pristine wilderness. Whether you are looking to relax, explore, or simply enjoy the stunning scenery, Ovahe Beach is a destination that promises to leave a lasting impression.

The Pink Sand Shores: One of the most striking features of Ovahe Beach is its pink sand, a rare and beautiful natural phenomenon that sets it apart from other beaches on the island. The sand gets its distinctive color from the crushed coral and volcanic minerals

that make up its composition, creating a soft, rosy hue that contrasts beautifully with the turquoise waters. Walking along the shores of Ovahe Beach is a sensory experience, as the soft sand cushions your feet and the sound of the waves soothes your soul. The pink sand shores are a perfect spot for a leisurely stroll or a quiet moment of reflection, where you can take in the beauty of your surroundings and feel at one with nature.

The Secluded Coves: Ovahe Beach is dotted with small, secluded coves, each offering its own unique charm and beauty. These hidden treasures are perfect for those looking to escape the crowds and enjoy a more intimate connection with nature. The coves are sheltered by the surrounding cliffs, creating a sense of privacy and seclusion. Here, you can find your own little slice of paradise, where the only sounds are the gentle lapping of the waves and the occasional call of a seabird. Whether you choose to swim, sunbathe, or simply relax in the shade, the coves of Ovahe Beach provide a peaceful retreat from the world.

The Cliffside Views: The cliffs that surround Ovahe Beach offer some of the most breathtaking views on Easter Island. These rugged cliffs, carved by the forces of nature over millennia, rise dramatically from the beach, creating a stunning contrast with the soft sands below. The views from the top of the cliffs are nothing short of spectacular, with panoramic vistas of the coastline and the endless expanse of the Pacific Ocean. The cliffs are also home to a variety of plant and bird species, adding to the natural beauty of the area. For those willing to take the short hike to the top, the reward is a view that will stay with you long after you leave the island.

The Crystal-Clear Waters: The waters around Ovahe Beach are some of the clearest on Easter Island, making it a popular spot for snorkeling and diving. The underwater world here is teeming with life, from colorful coral reefs to schools of tropical fish. The visibility is often excellent, allowing you to see the vibrant marine life in all its glory. Snorkeling in these waters is like entering a different world, where you can glide effortlessly among the coral gardens and observe the diverse ecosystem that thrives beneath the surface. For those who prefer to stay on dry land, the clear waters are also perfect for a refreshing swim or simply to admire from the shore.

The Untouched Wilderness: Ovahe Beach is one of the few places on Easter Island that remains largely untouched by human development. The beach and its surroundings are protected, preserving their natural beauty and ecological significance. This sense of wilderness is what makes Ovahe Beach so special, offering a rare opportunity to connect with nature in its purest form. The beach is a place of quiet contemplation, where you can feel the presence of the island's ancient past and the power of the natural world. Whether you are exploring the beach, hiking the cliffs, or simply sitting in the sand, Ovahe Beach is a place where you can find peace and inspiration.

4.11 Outdoor Activities and Adventures

Easter Island provides ample opportunities for exploration and adventure. From trekking through volcanic craters to snorkeling in crystal-clear waters, Easter

Island invites travelers to immerse themselves in its unique environment. Here are some of the top outdoor activities you can experience on this captivating island

Hiking the Rano Raraku Volcano: Rano Raraku, often referred to as the Moai quarry, is a must-visit destination for outdoor enthusiasts. Located on the southeastern coast of Easter Island, this volcanic crater is where the iconic Moai statues were carved from volcanic tuff. Hiking around Rano Raraku offers a fascinating journey through history and geology. The trail meanders past partially finished Moai statues, providing a unique glimpse into the island's ancient carving techniques. The hike is moderately challenging but rewarding, with panoramic views of the surrounding landscape from the crater rim. Admission to the site typically costs around $80 USD, which also grants access to other significant archaeological sites on the island. For more details and to plan your visit, check the official website of the Easter Island Tourism Office at (https://rapanuiexplorer.com).

Snorkeling at Anakena Beach: Anakena Beach is not only famous for its historical significance but also for its beautiful snorkeling opportunities. Located on the northern coast of Easter Island, this pristine beach features clear turquoise waters and a vibrant underwater world. The coral reefs here are home to a variety of marine life, including colorful fish and occasional sea turtles. The calm, shallow waters make it an ideal spot for snorkelers of all experience levels. Local operators offer snorkeling tours, which generally cost around $60 USD per person. These tours often include equipment rental and guidance from experienced instructors. For more information on snorkeling tours and other beach activities, visit the official website of Easter Island Adventures at (https://easterislandadventures.com).

Exploring the Orongo Ceremonial Village: The Orongo Ceremonial Village, situated atop the Rano Kau crater, is a fascinating site for those interested in cultural history and dramatic landscapes. The village was once the center of the Birdman cult, a unique religious practice of the Rapa Nui people. Hiking through Orongo provides a glimpse into the ceremonial life of the island's ancient inhabitants, with well-preserved stone houses and petroglyphs depicting the Birdman and other symbols. The trek to Orongo is a moderate hike with stunning views of the crater lake and surrounding islets. Admission to the site is usually included in a combined ticket for various archaeological sites, costing around $80 USD. Detailed visitor information can be found on the Rapa Nui National Park's official website at (https://rapanuinationalpark.com).

Horseback Riding Across the Island: For a different perspective of Easter Island's landscape, consider a horseback riding tour. These tours take you across diverse terrains, from the lush valleys to the rugged coastline. Located near Hanga Roa, several local operators offer guided horseback riding experiences that range from a few hours to full-day adventures. These rides provide an immersive experience into the island's natural beauty, including visits to lesser-known Moai sites and scenic viewpoints. Prices for horseback riding tours typically start around $100 USD per person and include equipment, safety instructions, and a local guide. To book a ride and find more information, visit the official website of Easter Island Horse Riding at (https://easterislandhorseriding.com).

Kayaking and Stand-Up Paddleboarding: Easter Island's clear, calm waters are perfect for kayaking and stand-up paddleboarding. These activities offer a serene way to explore the island's coastline and enjoy its natural beauty from the water. Popular spots for these water activities include the calm bays around Hanga Roa and the picturesque shores of Anakena Beach. Rental services and guided tours are available, with prices starting around $50 USD for a few hours of kayaking or paddleboarding. Equipment rental typically includes safety gear and a brief introduction to the activity. For more details on rentals and guided tours, visit the official website of Easter Island Kayak Tours at (https://easterislandkayaktours.com).

4.12 Guided Tours and Recommended Tour Operators

Exploring Easter Island's rich cultural heritage and stunning landscapes is best done with the help of knowledgeable local guides. Several tour operators on the island offer specialized guided tours that cater to various interests, from historical explorations to adventurous activities. Each operator brings its own unique flavor to the island experience, ensuring that visitors can find a tour that suits their preferences and enhances their understanding of this remote paradise.

Explora Rapa Nui: Explora Rapa Nui is renowned for its luxurious and immersive travel experiences. Located in Hanga Roa, the tour operator specializes in high-end guided tours that offer an in-depth exploration of Easter Island's cultural and natural wonders. Their tours are all-inclusive, covering transportation, meals, and expert guides who provide detailed insights into the island's history and landmarks. The company offers various tour packages, including private excursions and group tours. Prices typically start at around $800 USD per person for a multi-day package. For more details on their offerings, visit the official website of Explora Rapa Nui at (https://explora.com).

Easter Island Travel: Easter Island Travel, based in Hanga Roa, offers a range of guided tours that cater to different interests and budgets. Their tours include visits to iconic sites such as the Moai statues, Rano Raraku, and Orongo, as well as more specialized experiences like snorkeling and cultural workshops. The company provides both group and private tour options, with prices starting around $150 USD for half-day tours. Their knowledgeable guides are well-versed in the island's history and traditions, ensuring an enriching experience. For more information and to book a tour, check out the official website of Easter Island Travel at (https://easterisland.travel).

Rapa Nui Tours: Rapa Nui Tours, located in the heart of Hanga Roa, is known for its personalized and flexible tour options. They offer a variety of guided excursions that can be customized to fit the interests and schedules of their clients. From historical and archaeological tours to adventure activities, Rapa Nui Tours provides comprehensive services with a focus on customer satisfaction. Prices for their tours vary, starting at approximately $200 USD for a full-day private tour. For more details and to arrange a tour, visit the official website of Rapa Nui Tours at (https://rapanuitours.com).

Moto Nui Tours: Moto Nui Tours specializes in eco-friendly and cultural tours that emphasize sustainable travel practices. Based in Hanga Roa, the company offers a range of guided excursions that highlight the island's natural beauty and cultural heritage. Their tours include visits to remote Moai sites, eco-trekking adventures, and cultural experiences with local artisans. Prices for Moto Nui Tours start at around $180 USD per person for a half-day tour. Their commitment to environmental conservation and cultural preservation makes them a great choice for responsible travelers. For more information, visit the official website of Moto Nui Tours at (https://motonuitours.com).

CHAPTER 5
PRACTICAL INFORMATION AND GUIDANCE

5.1 Maps and Navigation

MAP OF EASTER ISLAND

SCAN THE QR CODE WITH A DEVICE TO VIEW A COMPREHENSIVE AND LARGER MAP OF EASTER ISLAND

Exploring Easter Island, or Rapa Nui, is an adventure that takes you through a land steeped in mystery, culture, and breathtaking natural beauty. To truly experience this remote island in the Pacific, having reliable maps and navigation tools is essential. Whether you prefer the tactile feel of a paper map or the convenience of a digital one, knowing how to access and utilize these resources can enhance your journey and ensure you don't miss a single wonder that this enigmatic island has to offer.

The Tourist Map of Easter Island: When you set foot on Easter Island, one of the first tools you'll want to get your hands on is a comprehensive tourist map. This map serves as your gateway to exploring the island's rich tapestry of archaeological sites, volcanic craters, and coastal trails. A well-crafted paper map not only highlights key points of interest, such as the iconic moai statues, but also provides insights into the island's geography, cultural landmarks, and natural reserves. The paper map can often be obtained upon arrival at Mataveri International Airport, local tourist information centers, or from your hotel. These maps are typically designed with detailed legends and scales, making it easy to plan your route, whether you're hiking, biking, or driving. A paper map is invaluable for understanding the layout of Easter Island, giving you a tangible sense of its size and the distances between various attractions. It also serves as a beautiful keepsake, a memento of your travels that you can refer to long after you've left the island's shores.

Accessing Easter Island's Maps Offline: For those who cherish the charm of traditional navigation, paper maps are an excellent resource, but there's also a way to bridge the gap between traditional and modern by accessing maps offline through digital means. Before you even embark on your journey to Easter Island, it's wise to download offline maps to your smartphone or tablet. Applications such as Google Maps or Maps.me offer the ability to save detailed maps of Easter Island that you can access without needing an internet connection. This is particularly useful given the island's remote location, where mobile signal can be sporadic, and Wi-Fi availability is limited to certain areas. To download an offline map, you simply need to search for Easter Island in the app while you have internet access, and select the option to download the area. Once saved, these maps will allow you to explore the island with GPS guidance even when you're off the grid. This method not only offers convenience but also peace of mind, ensuring that you won't lose your way, even in the most secluded corners of the island.

Digital Maps: Digital maps have become indispensable, especially for travelers who prefer to explore with the assistance of technology. Digital maps of Easter Island are available through various apps and platforms, offering detailed information on everything from the island's rugged trails to the location of cultural heritage sites. Using digital maps allows you to zoom in on specific areas, search for nearby attractions, and get real-time navigation to guide you from one site to the next. Moreover, digital maps often include user reviews, photos, and tips from fellow travelers, enhancing your experience with insider knowledge. Whether you're seeking the best viewpoint for sunset or trying to locate a hidden moai, digital maps can provide instant answers, making your exploration of Easter Island both efficient and enriching. For those who want to go a step further, this guide includes a QR code that directs you to a comprehensive digital map of Easter Island. This map is designed to be user-friendly and accessible from any device, offering a seamless way to plan your itinerary and navigate the island with confidence. Simply scan the QR code or click the link provided, and you'll have all of Easter Island's wonders at your fingertips.

Tips for Navigating Easter Island: Navigating Easter Island requires more than just a map; it calls for an understanding of the island's unique environment and cultural significance. Roads on the island are limited, and many of the most interesting sites are located off the beaten path, accessible only by foot or bike. It's essential to respect the island's natural and cultural heritage by sticking to marked paths and being mindful of the fragile ecosystems. Additionally, the island's small size means that you can explore most of it in just a few days, but taking your time to absorb the atmosphere of each location is highly recommended. Whether you're hiking up to Rano Kau crater, exploring the ancient village of Orongo, or marveling at the moai of Ahu Tongariki, a map will guide you, but your sense of curiosity and respect for the land will truly shape your journey.

5.2 Five Days Itinerary

Easter Island, with its enigmatic Moai statues, lush landscapes, and rich cultural heritage, offers an unforgettable travel experience. To make the most of your visit, it's essential to have a well-planned itinerary. This five-day guide provides a balanced mix of historical exploration, natural beauty, and cultural immersion, ensuring you experience the best of Rapa Nui.

Day 1: Arrival and Introduction to Hanga Roa

Arrive at Mataveri International Airport and check in to your accommodation in Hanga Roa, the island's main town. Take some time to settle in and familiarize yourself with your surroundings. Most hotels and guesthouses are conveniently located near the town center, making it easy to explore on foot.

Afternoon: Begin your adventure with a leisurely stroll around Hanga Roa. Visit the Museo Antropológico Sebastián Englert, which offers a comprehensive introduction to the island's history and culture. Here, you'll find exhibits on the Moai statues, Rapa Nui traditions, and archaeological artifacts. Enjoy a meal at a local restaurant, where you can sample traditional Rapa Nui cuisine such as po'e (a type of sweet potato pudding) or umukekeke (barbecued fish).

Evening: Head to the Tahai Archaeological Complex for your first sunset on the island. This site features several Moai statues, including some with their original red topknots. The combination of the ancient statues and the setting sun creates a breathtaking scene.

Day 2: The Moai Statues and Rano Raraku

Start your day with a visit to Rano Raraku, the quarry where the Moai statues were carved. This UNESCO World Heritage Site is home to nearly 400 Moai in various stages of completion. Walking through the quarry provides insight into the craftsmanship and effort involved in creating these iconic statues.

Afternoon: Continue your exploration to Ahu Tongariki, the largest ceremonial platform on the island, featuring 15 restored Moai statues. The site is impressive both for its historical significance and its stunning coastal location. In the afternoon, relax at Anakena Beach, a beautiful white sand beach that is also home to several Moai statues. The beach is perfect for swimming and sunbathing, offering a refreshing break from your archaeological explorations.

Evening: Return to Hanga Roa for dinner at one of the town's restaurants. Consider trying a local seafood dish or a traditional Rapa Nui feast.

Day 3: Discovering Orongo and Rano Kau

Head to the Orongo Ceremonial Village on the crater rim of Rano Kau. Orongo was the center of the Birdman Cult, which involved a unique competition to retrieve an egg from a seabird. The village features petroglyphs and remains of ceremonial structures that offer a glimpse into this fascinating aspect of Rapa Nui culture.

Afternoon: Explore the Rano Kau Crater, which is filled with a freshwater lake and surrounded by dramatic volcanic cliffs. The crater provides panoramic views of the island and is a great spot for photography.

Evening: Attend a traditional Rapa Nui cultural performance in the evening. Many local restaurants and cultural centers offer shows featuring traditional dance, music, and storytelling. This is an excellent opportunity to immerse yourself in the island's vibrant culture.

Day 4: Hiking and Scenic Views
Embark on a hike to the summit of Terevaka, the island's highest peak. The hike offers stunning panoramic views of Easter Island and the surrounding ocean. It's a moderately challenging trek, so bring plenty of water and wear sturdy footwear.

Afternoon: After descending from Terevaka, visit Ahu Akivi, a site known for its seven Moai statues that face the ocean. This site is unique because the statues are oriented towards the sea, unlike most others on the island.

Evening: Return to Hanga Roa and spend your evening relaxing. Enjoy dinner at a local restaurant and take a leisurely walk around town. Consider visiting the local artisan shops to purchase souvenirs.

Day 5: Final Explorations and Departure
Before departing, take a final tour of some lesser-visited sites such as Ahu Vaihu and Ahu Hanga Te'e. These sites offer additional perspectives on the island's archaeological sites and Moai statues.
Afternoon: Return to Hanga Roa for any last-minute shopping or sightseeing. Pick up souvenirs from local shops and enjoy a final meal at a restaurant of your choice.

Evening: Head to Mataveri International Airport for your departure. Reflect on the incredible experiences you've had during your stay on Easter Island and prepare for your journey home.

5.3 Essential Packing List

Traveling to Easter Island, one of the most remote inhabited places on Earth, requires thoughtful preparation and a well-considered packing list. This mystical island, known for its enigmatic moai statues and rich cultural history, offers a unique travel experience that blends natural beauty with ancient heritage. However, its isolation means that certain items are not readily available, and the unpredictable weather can present challenges for the unprepared. Ensuring you have everything you need not only enhances your comfort but also allows you to fully immerse yourself in the wonders of this fascinating destination.

Clothing for Every Occasion: The climate on Easter Island is subtropical, with temperatures that are generally mild throughout the year, but the weather can change rapidly, shifting from sunny skies to sudden downpours. As such, packing versatile clothing that can be layered is essential. Light, breathable fabrics are ideal for daytime exploration, as they keep you cool while you're hiking or visiting archaeological sites. A sturdy, wide-brimmed hat and sunglasses are also crucial for protecting yourself from the intense sun, especially during the island's warmer months. However, the evenings can be cooler, and it's wise to bring along a lightweight jacket or sweater. This not only provides warmth but also offers protection against the wind, which can be particularly strong near the coast. If you're visiting during the rainy season, which typically runs from May to August, a compact, waterproof jacket is a must-have. The island's trails and roads can become muddy and slippery, so waterproof footwear or hiking boots with good traction are highly recommended. These will keep your feet dry and provide stability on uneven terrain.

Essentials for Outdoor Exploration: Easter Island is a paradise for outdoor enthusiasts, with its rugged landscapes, volcanic craters, and coastal cliffs offering countless opportunities for adventure. To make the most of your time exploring the island, packing the right gear is crucial. A quality backpack is indispensable, serving as your day-to-day carryall for hikes and excursions. It should be spacious enough to hold your essentials, including water, snacks, sunscreen, and a first-aid kit, but also lightweight and comfortable to wear for extended periods. Given the island's limited infrastructure, bringing a reusable water bottle is essential. Staying hydrated while exploring is crucial, especially under the hot sun, and a refillable bottle allows you to carry sufficient water for your day's activities without relying on limited local resources. A pair of binoculars can also enhance your experience, particularly if you're interested in birdwatching or want to get a closer look at the distant moai statues.

Protecting Yourself from the Elements: Easter Island's isolation and natural environment mean that you'll be exposed to the elements for much of your visit. Protecting yourself from the sun is paramount, as the island's proximity to the equator means the sun's rays can be particularly harsh. In addition to a hat and sunglasses, pack a high-SPF sunscreen that is water-resistant and suitable for prolonged exposure. Reapply regularly, especially if you're swimming or sweating during hikes. Insect repellent is another essential, particularly if you're visiting during the wetter months when mosquitoes can be more prevalent. Choose a repellent that is effective against a wide range of insects to ensure you're protected while exploring the island's more remote areas. Aloe vera gel or after-sun lotion can also be a lifesaver if you do get sunburned, providing soothing relief for your skin.

Preparing for the Unexpected: Traveling to such a remote location requires a certain level of self-sufficiency, as medical facilities and pharmacies are limited on Easter Island. It's important to pack a well-stocked first-aid kit that includes basics like band-aids, antiseptic wipes, pain relievers, and any prescription medications you may need. Consider adding motion sickness tablets if you plan on taking a boat trip or exploring the island's rugged coastline, where the waters can be choppy. Bringing your own toiletries is also advisable, as the selection on the island can be limited and expensive. Include items like shampoo, conditioner, toothpaste, and any personal hygiene products you might need. While some accommodations may provide these basics, having your own ensures you're not caught short if they don't.

Capturing the Memories: Easter Island is a destination that lends itself to photography, with its dramatic landscapes and iconic statues offering countless opportunities for stunning shots. Make sure to bring a reliable camera with plenty of memory cards and batteries, as these can be hard to find on the island. A tripod can also be useful, particularly for capturing the moai at sunrise or sunset when the lighting is at its most spectacular. If you prefer to use your smartphone for photography, consider bringing a portable power bank to keep it charged throughout the day. The island's remote locations can drain your battery quickly, especially if you're using GPS or other apps. A protective case for your phone is also advisable, as the rugged terrain and occasional rain can pose a risk to unprotected devices.

5.4 Setting Your Travel Budget

Embarking on a journey to Easter Island requires not only a sense of adventure but also careful financial planning. Setting a travel budget that aligns with your goals ensures a stress-free experience. Easter Island, with its remote location, can be an expensive destination, so it's essential to understand the cost landscape and plan accordingly. Whether you're drawn by the island's mysterious moai statues or its rich cultural heritage, a well-thought-out budget will allow you to make the most of your visit without unexpected financial strain.

Accommodation and Transportation: Accommodation and transportation are among the most significant costs you'll face when visiting Easter Island. Flights to this remote island are primarily serviced by LATAM Airlines from Santiago, Chile, or Tahiti, and they can be pricey, especially during peak seasons. Booking your flights well in advance and considering the timing of your visit can help you manage these costs. Similarly, accommodation options on the island range from budget hostels to luxury lodges, all of which can be more expensive than mainland equivalents due to the cost of transporting goods to the island. To explore the island's wonders at your own pace, renting a vehicle is the most common option, though this too should be factored into your budget.

Dining on Easter Island: Food on Easter Island is another considerable expense, given that nearly all food products are imported. Dining out can be costly, but there are ways to enjoy the island's culinary offerings while managing your budget. Purchasing groceries and preparing some meals on your own can significantly reduce costs, especially if your accommodation includes kitchen facilities. Additionally, local markets and small eateries offer fresh, affordable options that allow you to sample the island's flavors without overspending. Balancing self-catering with occasional dining out can provide both a cultural experience and a way to stay within your budget.

Exploring Easter Island: The primary draw of Easter Island is its archaeological sites, and exploring these requires careful budgeting. Guided tours, while insightful and often necessary to fully appreciate the island's history, can be expensive. Group tours offer a more affordable way to experience the key sites, but entrance fees to Rapa Nui National Park should also be included in your budget. Planning your activities in advance, prioritizing must-see sites, and considering the cost of additional activities like snorkeling or horseback riding will help you allocate your budget effectively.

Miscellaneous Expenses: No travel budget is complete without accounting for miscellaneous expenses, which can quickly add up on Easter Island. Whether it's souvenir shopping, tipping, or unexpected costs like emergency supplies, these small expenses can impact your overall budget if not planned for. Setting aside a portion of your budget for these costs ensures that you can enjoy your trip without financial surprises. Additionally, having some cash on hand for tips or small purchases can be helpful, as not all places on the island accept credit cards. By planning for these miscellaneous expenses, you'll be prepared for anything your adventure on Easter Island might throw your way.

5.5 Visa Requirements and Entry Procedures

Easter Island, with its awe-inspiring Moai statues and rich cultural heritage, is a dream destination for many travelers. However, before you can set foot on this remote island, nestled in the vast Pacific Ocean, it's crucial to understand the visa requirements and entry procedures. This section will guide you through the process, whether you're arriving by air, train, or road, ensuring that your journey to Easter Island is as smooth as possible.

Visa Requirements: Easter Island is a special territory of Chile, and as such, the visa requirements for Easter Island are aligned with those for Chile. Depending on your nationality, you may or may not need a visa to enter Chile and subsequently Easter Island. Citizens of most countries in the Americas, Europe, and parts of Asia can enter Chile for up to 90 days without a visa. However, it's always advisable to check with the Chilean consulate or embassy in your home country before making travel plans, as visa requirements can change. For travelers who do require a visa, the process typically involves submitting an application to the Chilean consulate in your country of residence. You will need to provide a valid passport, a completed visa application form, proof of sufficient funds for your stay, and details of your accommodation on Easter Island. The visa process can take several weeks, so it's important to apply well in advance of your intended travel date.

Entry by Air: The vast majority of visitors to Easter Island arrive by air, flying from Santiago, Chile's capital city. LATAM Airlines operates regular flights between Santiago and Easter Island, a journey that takes approximately five and a half hours. As Easter Island is a remote destination, it's essential to book your flights well in advance, especially during peak travel seasons. When flying to Easter Island, you will first need to go through standard immigration procedures in Santiago if you are arriving from an international destination. This includes presenting your passport, visa (if required), and completing any necessary immigration forms. Once in Santiago, your flight to Easter Island is considered a domestic flight, so no additional visa checks are typically required. Upon arrival at Mataveri International Airport on Easter Island, visitors must complete a tourist card, which is typically issued during the flight. This card must be kept with you throughout your stay and will be collected when you leave the island. It's a straightforward process, but losing this card can cause delays when departing, so keep it in a safe place.

Entry by Sea: Although rare, some adventurous travelers choose to reach Easter Island by sea. This option is not for the faint of heart, as it requires significant planning and a strong spirit of adventure. There are no regular passenger ferries to Easter Island, so those arriving by sea usually do so via private yacht or as part of a specialized cruise. For those who do arrive by sea, immigration procedures are similar to those for air travelers. Upon docking at Easter Island, you will need to present your passport, visa (if required), and complete the necessary immigration forms. It's important to inform the local authorities of your arrival in advance, as Easter Island's small port can accommodate only a limited number of vessels at a time.

Exploring Entry by Road: Given Easter Island's location in the middle of the Pacific Ocean, entry by road is, of course, not possible. However, once on the island, you'll find that renting a car is one of the best ways to explore the various archaeological sites and natural wonders at your own pace. Car rentals are available at the airport and in the main town of Hanga Roa, offering a convenient way to get around.

Important Considerations for Your Journey: When planning your trip to Easter Island, it's essential to ensure that your passport is valid for at least six months beyond your planned departure date. Additionally, while there are no specific vaccination requirements for Easter Island, it's always a good idea to check with your healthcare provider before traveling, particularly if you plan to visit other parts of Chile or South America.

5.6 Safety Tips and Emergency Contacts

Easter Island, or Rapa Nui, is a destination that promises adventure, mystery, and unparalleled natural beauty. However, like any remote location, it also requires a certain level of preparedness to ensure a safe and enjoyable experience. This section provides essential safety tips and emergency contacts to help you navigate the island with confidence and peace of mind.

General Safety Tips for Easter Island Travelers
While Easter Island is generally a safe destination, its remote location and unique environment mean that travelers should take a few precautions:

Stay Hydrated and Protect Yourself from the Sun: The island's climate can be hot and sunny, especially during the summer months. Always carry water with you, wear sunscreen, and protect yourself with a hat and sunglasses.

Respect Local Customs and Regulations: Easter Island has strict regulations to protect its cultural and natural heritage. This includes rules about interacting with the Moai statues and visiting sacred sites. Always follow the guidelines provided by local authorities to avoid legal issues and preserve the island's treasures.

Be Cautious When Exploring Remote Areas: The island's rugged terrain and remote areas can be challenging to navigate. If you plan to hike or explore less-traveled paths, ensure that you have a reliable map, adequate supplies, and inform someone of your plans.

Avoid Walking Alone at Night: While violent crime is rare, it's always safer to avoid walking alone at night, especially in less populated areas. Stick to well-lit and populated areas when venturing out after dark.

Health and Medical Safety: Easter Island has limited medical facilities, so it's important to take some health precautions before and during your visit:

Bring Essential Medications: If you take regular medication, bring enough to last your entire trip, as pharmacies on the island may not stock all medicines.

Travel Insurance: Ensure you have comprehensive travel insurance that covers medical emergencies. In the unlikely event that you need specialized medical care, you may need to be evacuated to mainland Chile, which can be costly without insurance.

Emergency Medical Services: The main hospital on Easter Island, Hospital Hanga Roa, provides basic medical services. For more serious conditions, evacuation to Santiago may be necessary. Familiarize yourself with the location of the hospital and emergency contact numbers.

Emergency Contacts

Having the right contact information can make all the difference in an emergency. Here are the key emergency contacts to have on hand during your visit to Easter Island:

Police: For emergencies requiring police assistance, dial 133. The local police are well-trained and can assist with a range of issues, from lost items to more serious incidents.

Fire Department: In case of fire, dial 132. The island's fire services are equipped to handle both urban and wildfires.

Ambulance/Medical Emergency: For medical emergencies, dial 131. This will connect you to emergency medical services, including ambulance dispatch.

Hospital Hanga Roa: The main hospital can be contacted directly for non-emergency medical issues. It's advisable to visit the hospital if you need medical attention while on the island.

Local Embassy or Consulate: If you're facing legal issues or need assistance from your home country, contact your embassy or consulate. While there may not be a direct consular presence on Easter Island, representatives in Santiago can assist remotely.

5.7 Currency Exchange and Banking Services

Easter Island is part of Chile, and the official currency is the Chilean Peso (CLP). It is essential to be aware of the exchange rate between your home currency and the Chilean Peso to budget appropriately for your trip. As exchange rates fluctuate, it's a good idea to check the latest rates before traveling.

Local Currency Usage: While some places may accept US dollars or credit cards, most transactions are conducted in Chilean Pesos. It's advisable to carry some cash for smaller purchases, especially in more remote areas where card payments may not be accepted.

Banks and Financial Services

Easter Island has several banking options for visitors, though the range of services may be more limited compared to mainland Chile. Here are some notable banks and their services:

Banco Estado: This is one of the primary banks on the island, located in Hanga Roa. Banco Estado offers standard banking services including cash withdrawals, currency exchange, and account management. It is a reliable option for visitors needing to manage their finances while on the island.

Banco de Chile: Also situated in Hanga Roa, Banco de Chile provides similar services to Banco Estado, including ATMs for cash withdrawals and currency exchange. This bank is a good choice for those who prefer a well-known banking institution.

BICE Bank: While primarily serving local residents, BICE Bank in Hanga Roa offers banking services to visitors as well. They provide ATMs and basic financial transactions.

Santander: This bank, located in the town center, provides ATMs and essential banking services. It is part of a major banking network, so it may be a convenient choice for visitors who need reliable access to their funds.

Corpbanca: Located in Hanga Roa, Corpbanca offers basic banking services and ATMs. It is another option for visitors needing financial services during their stay.

Currency Exchange and ATMs

There are limited options for currency exchange on the island. The best places to exchange foreign currency are the banks mentioned above. It is advisable to exchange a portion of your money before arriving on the island to ensure you have enough local currency upon arrival.

ATMs: ATMs are available in Hanga Roa, but they may have limited operating hours or may run out of cash during busy periods. Ensure you carry sufficient cash to cover your needs, especially if you plan to explore more remote areas of the island where ATMs may not be accessible.

Tips for Managing Money on Easter Island
Notify Your Bank: Inform your bank of your travel plans to avoid any issues with your credit or debit cards. This will help prevent your card from being flagged for suspicious activity.

Carry Multiple Payment Methods: It's wise to carry both cash and credit/debit cards. While most establishments accept cards, having cash on hand is useful for smaller transactions and in areas where cards may not be accepted.

Be Aware of Fees: Check for any fees associated with ATM withdrawals or currency exchange both on and off the island. Some banks may charge international transaction fees or currency conversion fees.

Keep Your Money Secure: Use a money belt or a secure location to store cash and important documents. It's also advisable to keep a copy of your passport and travel documents in case of loss or theft.

5.8 Language, Communication and Useful Phrases

Understanding the linguistic landscape of Easter Island, and learning a few key phrases, will not only help you navigate your way around the island but also deepen your connection with its people and heritage.

The Linguistic Landscape: Easter Island is a territory of Chile, and as such, Spanish is the primary language spoken by its residents. Most of the island's population is bilingual, speaking both Spanish and Rapa Nui, the Polynesian language of the indigenous people. While Spanish will be sufficient for most of your interactions on the island, learning a few words of Rapa Nui can greatly enhance your experience. Rapa Nui, with its melodious tones and unique vocabulary, is central to the island's identity. It is used in traditional songs, dances, and ceremonies, and you'll find it woven into the fabric of everyday life. Street names, the names of the Moai statues, and other significant landmarks often have Rapa Nui names, so having some familiarity with the language will help you better understand and appreciate these cultural references.

Useful Spanish Phrases for Your Visit: Here are some essential Spanish phrases that will be particularly useful during your visit to Easter Island:

- *Hola, ¿cómo estás? (Hello, how are you?) – A friendly greeting to use when meeting people.*
- *Gracias (Thank you) – Show your appreciation for services or help.*
- *¿Dónde está...? (Where is...?) – Useful for asking directions, e.g., "¿Dónde está el Moai?" (Where is the Moai?).*
- *¿Cuánto cuesta? (How much does it cost?) – Essential for shopping or when paying for services.*
- *Perdón, no hablo español muy bien. (Sorry, I don't speak Spanish very well.) – Helpful if you're not fluent in Spanish.*

Key Rapa Nui Phrases to Connect with the Culture

While Spanish is widely spoken, knowing a few Rapa Nui phrases can be a meaningful way to connect with the island's culture and its people:

- *Iorana (Hello) – A traditional greeting in Rapa Nui, often accompanied by a smile.*
- *Maururu (Thank you) – Expressing gratitude in the local language.*
- *Aroha nui (Love) – A phrase that reflects the warm, welcoming spirit of the islanders.*
- *Ha'u mai (Come here) – Useful if you're inviting someone to join you.*
- *Pehe koe? (How are you?) – A polite way to inquire about someone's well-being.*

Communication Tips for Easter Island Visitors

When communicating with the locals on Easter Island, a few simple tips can go a long way:

Speak Slowly and Clearly: If you're speaking Spanish or using Rapa Nui phrases, speak slowly and clearly. The islanders are patient and will appreciate your efforts to communicate in their language.

Use Non-Verbal Cues: Gestures, facial expressions, and body language are universal tools that can help convey your message, especially if there's a language barrier.

Be Respectful of Cultural Differences: Easter Island has a distinct culture that is different from mainland Chile and the rest of the world. Approach interactions with respect and openness, and be mindful of cultural sensitivities.

5.9 Shopping on Easter Island

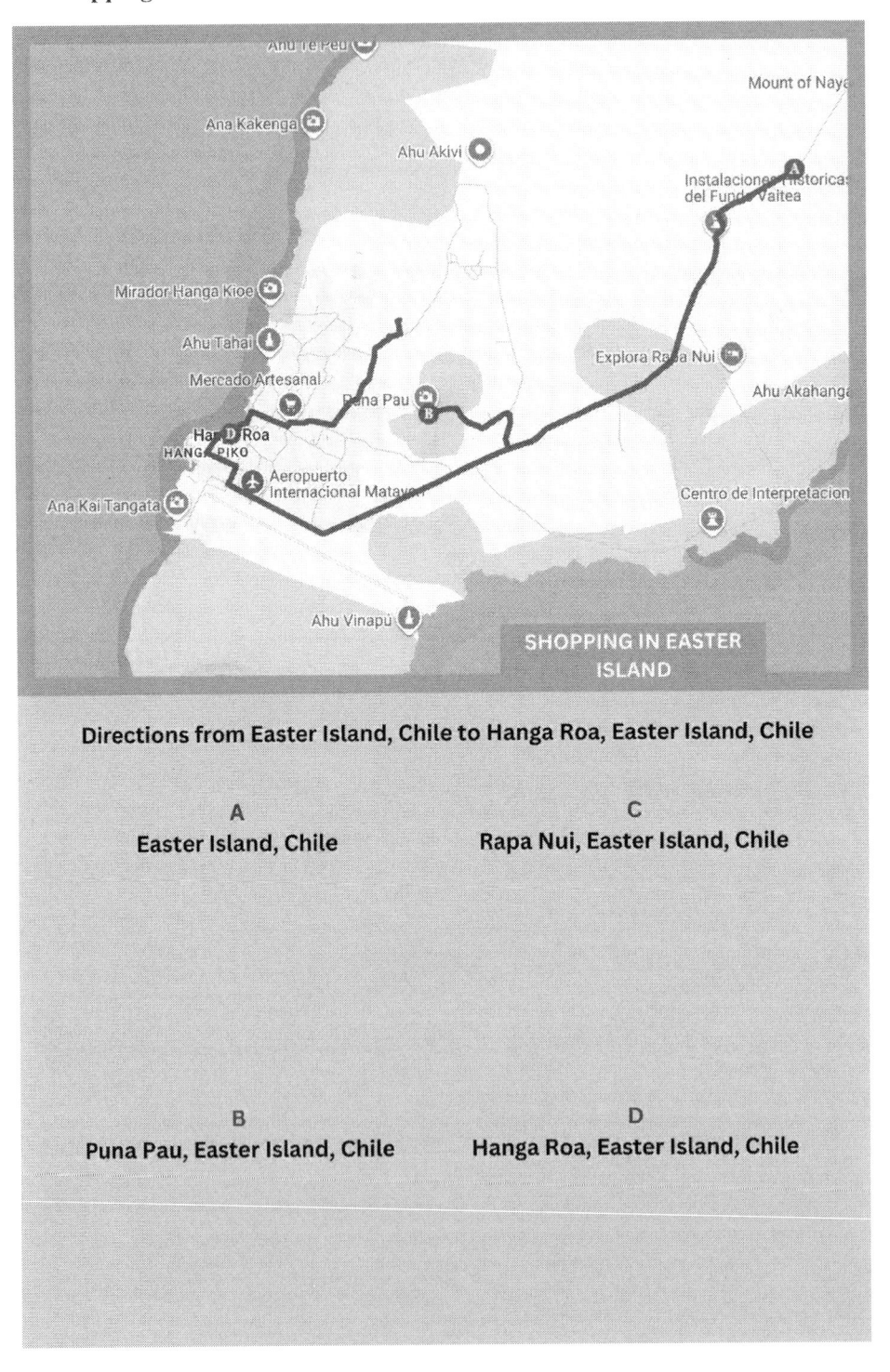

Directions from Easter Island, Chile to Hanga Roa, Easter Island, Chile

A
Easter Island, Chile

C
Rapa Nui, Easter Island, Chile

B
Puna Pau, Easter Island, Chile

D
Hanga Roa, Easter Island, Chile

Easter Island offers a unique shopping experience that reflects its heritage and artistry. From charming boutiques to intriguing antique stores, the island provides a variety of options for visitors looking to bring home a piece of Rapa Nui. This guide delves into notable shopping destinations on Easter Island, each offering a distinct selection of goods and souvenirs.

Boutique Stores

Puna Pau Gallery: Puna Pau Gallery, located centrally in Hanga Roa, is a must-visit for anyone interested in high-quality, locally crafted souvenirs. This boutique store specializes in traditional Rapa Nui art, including handcrafted Moai replicas, intricate carvings, and vibrant paintings that capture the island's essence. The gallery's offerings also include beautiful textiles and jewelry made by local artisans. Prices here range from $20 for smaller items such as keychains to over $300 for larger art pieces. The gallery is open daily from 9 AM to 6 PM, making it a convenient stop for both early and late shoppers. Its central location ensures easy access, and its curated collection provides an authentic taste of Easter Island's artistic heritage.

Ariki Arts and Crafts: Ariki Arts and Crafts is another gem located in Hanga Roa. This boutique focuses on authentic Rapa Nui crafts, featuring a wide array of handmade items including traditional wooden carvings, woven baskets, and locally made pottery. The store's collection reflects the island's rich cultural traditions, offering visitors a chance to purchase truly unique souvenirs. Prices here vary, with smaller crafts starting around $15 and larger, more intricate pieces priced up to $250. Ariki Arts and Crafts operates from 10 AM to 5 PM daily, providing ample opportunity for shoppers to explore its diverse selection. The store's knowledgeable staff can offer insights into the significance of the items, enhancing your shopping experience.

Antique Stores

Rapa Nui Antiques: For those interested in exploring historical artifacts, Rapa Nui Antiques offers a fascinating selection of vintage items and relics from the island's past. Located slightly off the beaten path in Hanga Roa, this store features an array of antiques, including old photographs, traditional tools, and historical documents. The collection provides a glimpse into the island's rich history and cultural evolution. Prices vary widely depending on the item's rarity and historical value, with smaller artifacts starting around $30 and more significant pieces reaching several hundred dollars. Rapa Nui Antiques is open from 11 AM to 4 PM daily, and its somewhat secluded location adds to the sense of discovery as you explore its treasures.

Souvenir Shops

Easter Island Souvenirs: Easter Island Souvenirs, located near the main square of Hanga Roa, is a popular spot for visitors seeking a wide range of mementos. This shop offers a diverse selection of items, including Moai statues, traditional masks, and colorful textiles. The store's extensive inventory ensures that there is something for everyone, whether you're looking for a small keepsake or a more substantial souvenir. Prices here are generally affordable, with items starting around $10 for small trinkets and going up to $100 or more for larger pieces. The shop is open from 9 AM to 7 PM daily, making it a convenient choice for last-minute shopping. Its central location makes it easy to find, and its wide range of products caters to various tastes and budgets.

Cultura Rapanui: Cultura Rapanui, located just a short walk from the central market, offers a blend of traditional and modern souvenirs. This shop features an assortment of handcrafted items, including intricately designed jewelry, traditional clothing, and art pieces. Cultura Rapanui is known for its emphasis on supporting local artisans, and many of its products are made using traditional techniques. Prices range from $20 for small items to over $200 for elaborate artworks and garments. The shop operates from 10 AM to 6 PM daily, providing ample time to explore its collection. With its focus on quality and authenticity, Cultura Rapanui is a great place to find both traditional and contemporary Rapa Nui goods.

5.10 Health and Wellness Centers

Easter Island offers a variety of health and wellness centers where visitors can rejuvenate their minds and bodies. These centers cater to a range of wellness needs, from relaxing massages to holistic treatments, allowing travelers to enhance their experience on this remote island. Here is an extensive overview of five notable health and wellness centers that provide exceptional services to ensure a revitalizing visit to Rapa Nui.

The Sacred Spa: The Sacred Spa, situated in the heart of Hanga Roa, offers an oasis of tranquility for those seeking a deep sense of relaxation and well-being. This center is renowned for its range of spa treatments, including therapeutic massages, aromatic baths, and traditional Rapa Nui healing practices. The

Sacred Spa utilizes local ingredients and techniques, integrating the island's natural resources into its treatments. Visitors can indulge in soothing massages designed to alleviate stress and tension, while the aromatic baths offer a revitalizing experience using locally sourced herbs and essential oils. The spa operates daily from 9 AM to 7 PM, providing flexible appointment options to accommodate various schedules. Guests can book treatments in advance through their website or by contacting the spa directly. The serene ambiance of the Sacred Spa, combined with its expert therapists, makes it an ideal destination for those seeking to unwind and rejuvenate during their island stay.

Ahu Wellness Retreat: Ahu Wellness Retreat, located slightly outside Hanga Roa amidst lush tropical surroundings, specializes in holistic health practices that focus on balancing mind, body, and spirit. This retreat offers a variety of services including yoga classes, meditation sessions, and nutritional counseling. The center is dedicated to promoting overall well-being through a comprehensive approach that incorporates physical exercise, mental relaxation, and healthy eating. Daily yoga classes cater to all skill levels, providing a peaceful environment for visitors to connect with their inner selves while enjoying the natural beauty of Easter Island. Meditation sessions, led by experienced instructors, offer tools and techniques for achieving mental clarity and emotional balance. Additionally, the retreat provides personalized nutritional advice, helping guests make informed choices about their diet and lifestyle. Ahu Wellness Retreat operates from 8 AM to 6 PM, with classes and sessions available throughout the day. Reservations can be made online or by phone, ensuring that visitors can secure their preferred times.

Rapa Nui Healing Center: Rapa Nui Healing Center blends traditional Rapa Nui healing methods with modern therapeutic practices, offering a unique wellness experience on the island. Located in Hanga Roa, this center provides a range of treatments that include traditional herbal remedies, acupuncture, and reflexology. The center's focus on combining indigenous practices with contemporary techniques creates a holistic approach to health and wellness. Guests can explore traditional Rapa Nui remedies, such as herbal poultices and plant-based treatments, which have been used for generations to address various ailments and promote well-being. Modern therapies, including acupuncture and reflexology, complement these traditional methods, providing a comprehensive approach to health. The Rapa Nui Healing Center is open daily from 10 AM to 5 PM, with appointments available by reservation. The center's practitioners are skilled in both traditional and modern techniques, ensuring a well-rounded experience for visitors seeking diverse therapeutic options.

Moai Wellness Center: Moai Wellness Center, located in the bustling center of Hanga Roa, offers a blend of fitness and relaxation services designed to cater to diverse wellness needs. The center features a fully equipped gym, group fitness classes, and a relaxing wellness area with a sauna and steam room. Moai Wellness Center's facilities are ideal for those looking to maintain their fitness routine while enjoying the island's unique environment. The gym is equipped with modern exercise equipment, and fitness classes range from high-intensity workouts to gentle stretching sessions, providing options for all levels of fitness enthusiasts. The wellness area, complete with a sauna and steam room, offers a relaxing retreat after a workout. Moai Wellness Center operates from 6 AM to 8 PM daily, allowing visitors to incorporate wellness into their daily routine. Memberships and day passes are available, and reservations for fitness classes can be made in advance.

Orito's Wellness Oasis: Orito's Wellness Oasis, a charming retreat located near the scenic coastline of Easter Island, specializes in personalized care and relaxation. This center offers a variety of services including bespoke massages, skincare treatments, and wellness consultations tailored to individual needs. Orito's Wellness Oasis is known for its intimate setting and personalized approach, ensuring that each guest receives attentive care and customized treatments. Massage therapies at Orito's Wellness Oasis are designed to address specific needs, from deep tissue massages to soothing relaxation techniques. Skincare treatments utilize high-quality products to nourish and revitalize the skin, while wellness consultations provide personalized advice on maintaining overall health and well-being. The center operates from 9 AM to 6 PM daily, with appointments available by reservation. Its tranquil location and focus on personalized care make it an excellent choice for visitors seeking a tailored wellness experience.

5.11 Useful Websites, Mobile Apps and Online Resources

Embarking on a journey to Easter Island, with its remote and enigmatic allure, requires thoughtful planning and preparation. To enhance the visitor experience, leveraging useful websites, mobile apps, and online resources can provide invaluable assistance in navigating the island's attractions, accommodations, and logistical needs. This guide delves into five essential digital tools that can enrich your visit to Easter Island, offering practical information and connectivity to ensure a seamless and enjoyable experience.

Discovering the "Easter Island Travel Guide" App: The "Easter Island Travel Guide" app is an indispensable resource for anyone exploring this remote destination. Designed specifically for travelers, this app provides a comprehensive overview of the island's attractions, historical sites, and practical information. With detailed maps and descriptions of key landmarks, including the Moai statues, volcanic craters, and archaeological sites, users can easily navigate the island and plan their itinerary. One of the standout features of the app is its offline functionality. Given the limited connectivity options on the island, having access to detailed maps and guides without relying on a constant internet connection is invaluable. The app also includes user reviews, practical tips, and recommendations for local dining and accommodations, making it a versatile tool for both planning and on-the-go assistance.

Navigating Local Transportation with "Moai Map" App: For those looking to explore Easter Island's diverse attractions, the "Moai Map" app offers an interactive and user-friendly way to manage local transportation and navigation. This app provides detailed maps with information on key points of interest, including bus stops, taxi services, and rental car agencies. The GPS-enabled functionality ensures that users can easily find their way to various sites, from the famous Ahu platforms to the serene beaches. The "Moai Map" app also includes real-time updates on public transportation schedules and routes, which is particularly useful given the limited options for getting around the island. By using this app, visitors can optimize their travel plans and make the most of their time on Easter Island, ensuring that they reach each destination efficiently and conveniently.

Cultural Insights with the "Rapa Nui Culture" App: Understanding the rich cultural heritage of Easter Island enhances the travel experience, and the "Rapa Nui Culture" app provides an in-depth exploration of the island's history and traditions. This app features comprehensive information about the indigenous Rapa Nui people, their customs, mythology, and the historical significance of the Moai statues. The "Rapa Nui Culture" app offers audio guides and interactive content that bring the island's history to life. Users can access detailed descriptions of historical sites, listen to expert commentary, and view high-quality images and videos. This immersive approach helps visitors gain a deeper appreciation of the cultural and historical context of their surroundings, making their exploration more meaningful and educational.

Staying Informed with "Easter Island News" Website: Keeping up-to-date with local news and events can greatly enhance your visit to Easter Island. The "Easter Island News" website serves as a valuable resource for the latest information on island activities, cultural events, and any important updates affecting travelers. The website provides regular articles and announcements about local happenings, weather forecasts, and any potential travel advisories. Visitors can use this website to plan their itinerary around special events, festivals, and cultural activities taking place during their stay. Additionally, the "Easter Island News" website often features travel tips and practical advice for visitors, helping to ensure that travelers are well-informed and prepared for their trip.

5.12 Internet Access and Connectivity

Easter Island provides various internet access and connectivity options to ensure that visitors can stay connected while exploring this unique destination. Given the island's isolation, understanding the available options for internet access is crucial for those who need to stay in touch with the outside world, whether for work, travel arrangements, or sharing their experiences. Here is an extensive overview of the key internet access and connectivity options available on Easter Island, designed to help visitors navigate their connectivity needs during their stay.

Wi-Fi Connectivity at Hotels and Accommodations: Most hotels and accommodations on Easter Island offer Wi-Fi as a standard amenity. Whether you are staying at a luxury resort, a mid-range hotel, or a guesthouse, you can expect to find Wi-Fi available to guests. The quality and speed of the internet connection can vary depending on the establishment, with upscale resorts often providing high-speed access, while smaller, more remote accommodations might offer basic connectivity. It is advisable to check with your hotel in advance to confirm the availability of Wi-Fi and any potential charges associated with its use. For those staying in more remote or less developed accommodations, it may be useful to inquire about the Wi-Fi signal strength and reliability, as connectivity can sometimes be affected by the island's geographical conditions. Many hotels also provide Wi-Fi in common areas such as lobbies, restaurants, and lounges, making it possible to access the internet even if your room's connection is less reliable.

Public Wi-Fi Hotspots in Hanga Roa: Hanga Roa, the island's main town, offers several public Wi-Fi hotspots where visitors can connect to the internet. Cafés, restaurants, and some public spaces in Hanga Roa provide free Wi-Fi to patrons, making it a convenient option for those who need to access the internet while enjoying a meal or coffee. These hotspots are particularly useful for checking emails, updating social media, or browsing the web. While the availability of free Wi-Fi in public places is a great advantage, the quality of the connection can vary. Public networks may be slower or less secure compared to private connections, so visitors should exercise caution when accessing sensitive information. Using a VPN (Virtual Private Network) can enhance security while using public Wi-Fi hotspots.

Local SIM Cards and Mobile Data: For more flexible internet access, visitors can purchase local SIM cards with mobile data plans. Several local providers offer SIM cards that can be used in unlocked phones to access 3G or 4G LTE networks on the island. Purchasing a local SIM card is a practical solution for those who need reliable internet access on the go or prefer not to rely on Wi-Fi networks. Local SIM cards can be bought from various shops in Hanga Roa, including convenience stores and telecommunications outlets. When purchasing a SIM card, visitors should ensure their phones are unlocked and compatible with local networks. Data plans vary in terms of data limits and prices, so it is advisable to select a plan that best suits your needs, whether for occasional use or more extensive data requirements.

Internet Cafés and Public Access Points: Internet cafés are another option for visitors seeking internet access on Easter Island. These establishments provide computers with internet connectivity, allowing guests to browse the web, check emails, and print documents. Internet cafés are typically located in Hanga Roa and cater to both locals and tourists. While internet cafés offer a reliable connection, they may not always provide the same level of speed and comfort as private accommodations or modern Wi-Fi hotspots. It is also worth noting that hours of operation can vary, so it is a good idea to check the opening times in advance. Some internet cafés may also offer additional services, such as printing and scanning, which can be useful for travelers needing to handle work or travel documents.

Satellite Internet Services: Given the island's remote location, satellite internet services are also available for those needing reliable connectivity, particularly for extended stays or specific work requirements. Satellite internet provides a connection through satellite signals, offering coverage even in areas where traditional terrestrial networks may not reach. Visitors can arrange for satellite internet services through specialized providers who offer equipment rentals and installation. While this option can be more expensive compared to other connectivity solutions, it ensures a stable connection in more remote parts of the island. This can be especially beneficial for travelers who require consistent internet access for professional purposes or for staying in touch with family and friends.

5.13 Visitor Centers and Tourist Assistance

Easter Island offers several visitor centers and tourist assistance services to enhance the travel experience. These centers play a crucial role in providing information, support, and resources to ensure that visitors can fully enjoy their time on the island. This guide explores key visitor centers and their special services, offering a detailed overview to help travelers navigate and make the most of their journey to Rapa Nui.

Rapa Nui National Park Visitor Center: The Rapa Nui National Park Visitor Center, located in Hanga Roa, serves as the primary hub for information about the island's most famous sites and natural attractions. Positioned near the park's main entrance, this center provides essential services for visitors exploring the UNESCO World Heritage site. The staff at the visitor center are well-versed in the island's cultural and environmental significance, offering detailed maps, educational brochures, and guidance on exploring landmarks such as the Moai statues and volcanic craters. The center is open daily from 8 AM to 5 PM, ensuring that visitors can obtain information and assistance throughout their day of exploration. Additionally, the center offers guided tour bookings, providing visitors with the option to experience the island's sites with knowledgeable local guides. This service not only enriches the understanding of the island's history and significance but also ensures a more immersive experience. The Rapa Nui National Park Visitor Center is a crucial resource for anyone looking to delve into the island's rich cultural tapestry and natural beauty.

Hanga Roa Tourist Information Office: The Hanga Roa Tourist Information Office is conveniently located in the heart of the island's main town, making it an accessible and central resource for visitors. This office provides a wide range of services designed to facilitate a smooth and enjoyable stay. Visitors can obtain detailed information on local attractions, accommodations, dining options, and transportation services. The staff at the Tourist Information Office are knowledgeable about current events, local customs, and practical travel tips, making it an excellent starting point for any visit. Operating from 9 AM to 6 PM daily, the office also offers assistance with booking local tours, excursions, and activities. Whether you're interested in exploring archaeological sites, participating in cultural events, or simply finding the best local eateries, the Hanga Roa Tourist Information Office is equipped to provide valuable recommendations and support. The central location of the office ensures that visitors can easily drop by to gather information and make necessary arrangements during their stay.

Cultural Heritage Center: The Cultural Heritage Center, located near the main square in Hanga Roa, offers an in-depth look at the history and traditions of Easter Island. This center is dedicated to preserving and promoting Rapa Nui's unique cultural heritage through exhibits, educational programs, and interactive displays. Visitors can explore artifacts, historical documents, and multimedia presentations that provide insights into the island's ancient past and ongoing cultural practices. The Cultural Heritage Center operates from 10 AM to 4 PM daily, providing ample opportunity for visitors to engage with the island's rich history. The center also hosts workshops and cultural events, offering hands-on experiences such as traditional crafts, music, and dance. These programs provide visitors with a deeper appreciation of Rapa Nui's cultural legacy and contribute to a more meaningful connection with the island's heritage.

Moai Foundation Office: The Moai Foundation Office, situated in Hanga Roa, plays a crucial role in the preservation and study of Easter Island's iconic Moai statues. This office serves as a research and information center dedicated to the conservation efforts of these historic monuments. Visitors can learn about ongoing restoration projects, archaeological research, and the significance of the Moai statues through informative displays and presentations. Open from 9 AM to 5 PM daily, the Moai Foundation Office provides guided tours of restoration sites and educational talks about the Moai statues' cultural and historical importance. The office also offers opportunities for visitors to contribute to preservation efforts through donations or volunteer programs. Engaging with the Moai Foundation Office allows visitors to gain a deeper understanding of the island's most famous landmarks and the efforts required to protect them for future generations.

Easter Island Eco-Tourism Center: The Easter Island Eco-Tourism Center, located on the outskirts of Hanga Roa, is dedicated to promoting sustainable travel practices and environmental conservation. This center provides information on eco-friendly tours, conservation initiatives, and ways for visitors to minimize their environmental impact while exploring the island. The center's focus on sustainability is reflected in its educational programs, which cover topics such as local wildlife protection, waste management, and the preservation of natural landscapes. Operating from 8 AM to 6 PM daily, the Eco-Tourism Center offers a range of services, including eco-tour bookings, educational workshops, and conservation volunteer opportunities. Visitors can learn about sustainable travel practices and participate in activities that support the island's environmental goals. The center's commitment to promoting responsible tourism ensures that visitors can enjoy Easter Island's beauty while contributing to its preservation.

CHAPTER 6
GASTRONOMIC DELIGHTS

6.1 Dining Options and Top Restaurants

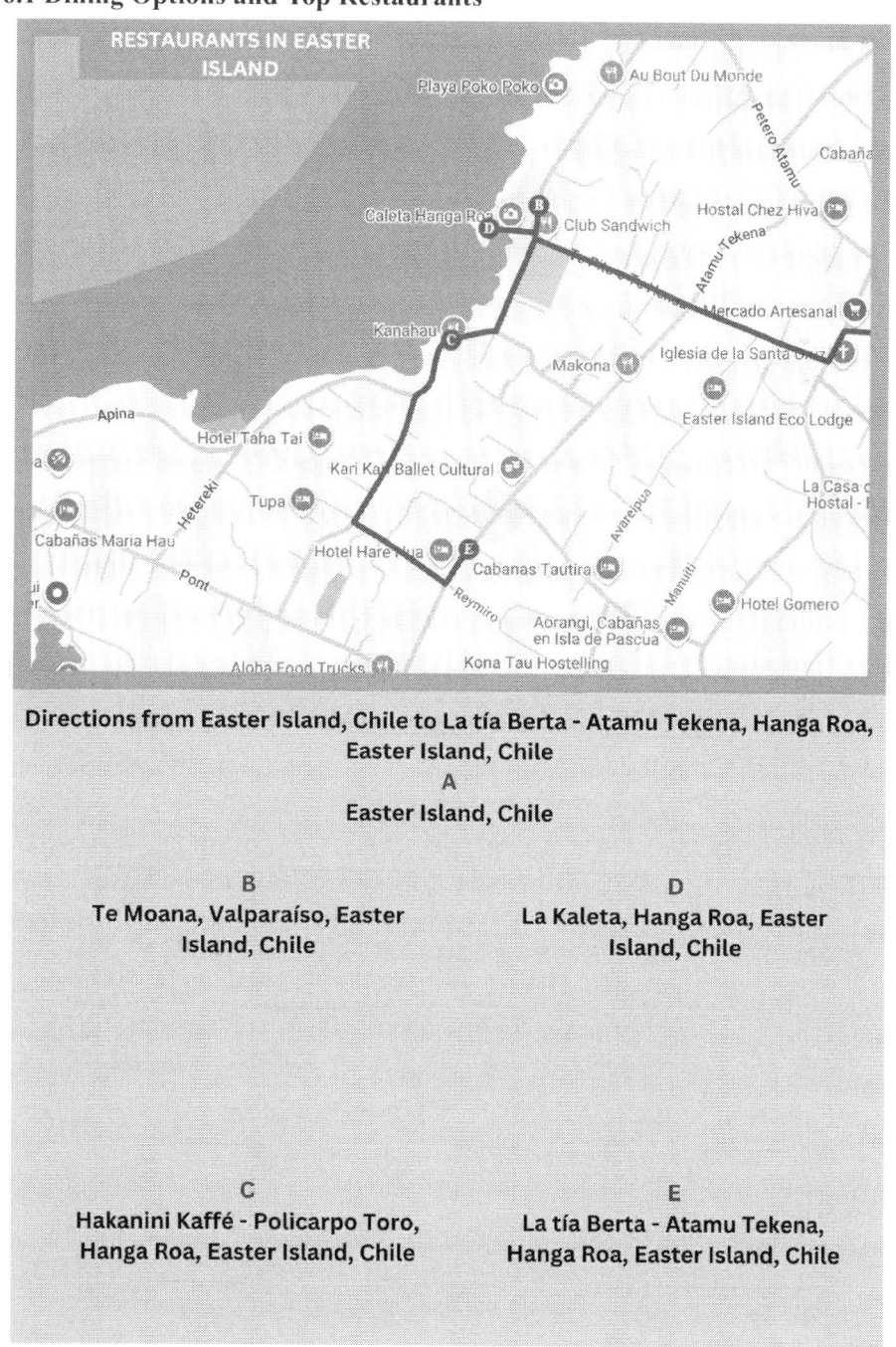

Directions from Easter Island, Chile to La tía Berta - Atamu Tekena, Hanga Roa, Easter Island, Chile

A
Easter Island, Chile

B
Te Moana, Valparaíso, Easter Island, Chile

D
La Kaleta, Hanga Roa, Easter Island, Chile

C
Hakanini Kaffé - Policarpo Toro, Hanga Roa, Easter Island, Chile

E
La tía Berta - Atamu Tekena, Hanga Roa, Easter Island, Chile

Easter Island also boasts a diverse and intriguing culinary scene. Whether you're seeking traditional Rapa Nui dishes or international cuisine with a local twist, the island offers a range of dining options that cater to various tastes and preferences. This guide delves into top restaurants and dining spots on Easter Island, providing detailed insights into their offerings, ambiance, and unique features.

Te Moana: Te Moana stands out as a premier dining destination on Easter Island, offering an exceptional blend of local and international cuisine. Located in the heart of Hanga Roa, this restaurant is renowned for its picturesque oceanfront setting, which provides diners with stunning views of the Pacific Ocean. The menu at Te Moana features a wide array of dishes, from fresh seafood and traditional Rapa Nui recipes to gourmet international fare. One of the highlights of Te Moana is its commitment to using fresh, locally sourced ingredients. The seafood dishes, including the celebrated Tuna Poke and Rongorongo, are particularly popular among visitors. The restaurant's elegant ambiance, combined with attentive service, makes it an ideal spot for a memorable dining experience. Prices at Te Moana typically range from 12,000 to 20,000 Chilean Pesos per dish, depending on the selection. For a truly unforgettable meal, consider making a reservation to secure a table with the best views of the sunset.

Haka Honu: Haka Honu offers a charming and authentic taste of Rapa Nui's culinary traditions, featuring a menu that celebrates local ingredients and recipes. Situated in Hanga Roa, this cozy restaurant is known for its warm and inviting atmosphere, making it a favorite among both locals and tourists. The menu at Haka Honu includes traditional dishes such as Kai Roroi and Po'e, as well as a selection of fresh seafood and grilled meats. The restaurant's dedication to preserving traditional flavors is evident in its carefully prepared dishes and use of locally sourced produce. Prices at Haka Honu are generally affordable, ranging from 6,000 to 12,000 Chilean Pesos per dish. Visitors can enjoy a relaxed dining experience, often accompanied by live music or cultural performances that add to the restaurant's vibrant ambiance. For an authentic taste of Rapa Nui, Haka Honu is a must-visit destination.

La Kaleta: La Kaleta offers a sophisticated dining experience with a focus on international cuisine, blending global flavors with local ingredients. Located in the center of Hanga Roa, this upscale restaurant features a diverse menu that includes everything from gourmet steaks and pasta dishes to innovative seafood creations. The chic and modern interior of La Kaleta provides a stylish setting for diners looking to enjoy a refined meal. One of the standout features of La Kaleta is its extensive wine list, which includes both local Chilean wines and international selections. The restaurant's commitment to high-quality ingredients and creative presentations makes it a popular choice for special occasions. Prices at La Kaleta typically range from 15,000 to 25,000 Chilean Pesos per dish, reflecting the restaurant's upscale offerings. Reservations are recommended, especially during peak dining hours, to ensure a table in this sought-after establishment.

Resto Bar Tia Berta: Resto Bar Tia Berta is a beloved local eatery that offers a casual and friendly atmosphere, perfect for enjoying traditional Rapa Nui fare. Located in Hanga Roa, this family-owned restaurant is known for its hearty and flavorful dishes, including local favorites such as Uru and freshly prepared seafood. The menu at Resto Bar Tia Berta features generous portions and affordable prices, making it a popular choice for both locals and visitors. The restaurant's rustic decor and laid-back vibe create a welcoming environment where diners can enjoy a relaxed meal. Prices at Resto Bar Tia Berta typically range from 5,000 to 10,000 Chilean Pesos per dish, providing excellent value for money. The restaurant's friendly staff and authentic Rapa Nui cuisine make it a great spot for experiencing the island's culinary traditions in a casual setting.

Ona Kena: Ona Kena is a seafood-centric restaurant that specializes in fresh and flavorful dishes inspired by Rapa Nui's maritime heritage. Situated near the waterfront in Hanga Roa, this dining spot offers breathtaking views of the ocean, enhancing the overall dining experience. The menu at Ona Kena includes a variety of seafood options, such as grilled fish, ceviche, and seafood stews, all prepared with a focus on freshness and quality. The restaurant's modern and stylish decor complements its emphasis on high-quality ingredients and inventive presentations. Prices at Ona Kena typically range from 8,000 to 15,000 Chilean Pesos per dish, reflecting the premium nature of the seafood offerings. For a memorable meal with a view, Ona Kena is an excellent choice, and making a reservation is advisable to secure a table with the best ocean views.

6.2 Cafes and Food Trucks

These casual spots offer a different taste of island life, with quick bites, refreshing beverages, and local flavors served in a relaxed setting. Whether you're looking for a morning coffee, a light snack, or a flavorful lunch on the go, the island's cafés and food trucks provide diverse options for visitors. Here's a closer look at popular choices for a delightful culinary experience on Easter Island.

Café Tupa: Café Tupa, located in the heart of Hanga Roa, is a beloved spot for coffee enthusiasts and casual diners alike. This cozy café offers a welcoming atmosphere with its colorful décor and comfortable seating, making it an ideal place to unwind with a cup of coffee or enjoy a light meal. Café Tupa is renowned for its freshly brewed coffee, which is made from locally sourced beans and expertly crafted by skilled baristas. The menu at Café Tupa features a range of options, including pastries, sandwiches, and salads. The café's signature offerings include the Tupa Special Coffee and homemade pastries like croissants and empanadas. Prices are reasonable, with coffee starting at around 3,000 Chilean Pesos and pastries priced between 2,000 and 4,000 Chilean Pesos. For a relaxed break during your island exploration, Café Tupa provides a perfect blend of quality coffee and a friendly atmosphere.

Heladería Rapa Nui: Heladería Rapa Nui is a popular food truck that specializes in delicious ice creams and frozen treats. Positioned in a central location in Hanga Roa, this vibrant food truck offers a variety of flavors, including local fruit-based options and classic favorites. The ice creams at Heladería Rapa Nui are made from high-quality ingredients, and the truck's unique flavors provide a refreshing way to cool down on a warm island day. The food truck's menu features an array of ice cream flavors, including exotic options like passion fruit and guava, as well as traditional choices like vanilla and chocolate. Prices for ice cream start at around 2,000 Chilean Pesos for a small cone, with larger servings available for a bit more. Heladería Rapa Nui's convenient location and delectable treats make it a popular choice for a sweet snack while exploring the island.

Food Truck La Isla Bonita: Food Truck La Isla Bonita is a local favorite that offers a diverse menu of tasty street food, combining traditional Rapa Nui flavors with international influences. Located near popular tourist spots in Hanga Roa, this food truck serves up a variety of dishes, including tacos, empanadas, and grilled meats. The vibrant and colorful setup of the truck adds to its appeal, attracting visitors with its inviting aroma and lively atmosphere. The menu at Food Truck La Isla Bonita features flavorful options such as Tacos de Pescado (fish tacos) and Carne Asada (grilled beef). Prices are affordable, with most dishes priced between 3,000 and 6,000 Chilean Pesos. The food truck's convenient location and flavorful offerings make it an excellent choice for a quick and satisfying meal while on the go.

Café El Ombligo: Café El Ombligo offers a unique blend of traditional Rapa Nui cuisine and international dishes in a relaxed café setting. Situated in Hanga Roa, this café provides a charming atmosphere with its rustic decor and friendly service. The menu features a range of options, including local favorites like Ceviche and traditional Chilean sandwiches, as well as international fare such as pasta and burgers. One of the highlights of Café El Ombligo is its emphasis on using fresh, local ingredients to prepare its dishes. The café's menu items are priced between 4,000 and 8,000 Chilean Pesos, making it an affordable option for a casual meal or snack. With its inviting ambiance and diverse menu, Café El Ombligo is a great spot to enjoy a laid-back meal while soaking in the island's relaxed atmosphere.

Café Ariki: Café Ariki is a charming café that blends local flavors with creative culinary twists. Located in a bustling area of Hanga Roa, this café is known for its innovative approach to traditional Rapa Nui dishes and its welcoming atmosphere. The menu at Café Ariki includes a range of options, from artisanal coffee and fresh juices to light meals like quiches and salads. The café's commitment to using locally sourced ingredients and its creative menu offerings make it a standout choice for visitors seeking a unique dining experience. Prices at Café Ariki generally range from 3,500 to 7,000 Chilean Pesos, depending on the dish. The café's vibrant decor and friendly service enhance the overall dining experience, making it a popular spot for both locals and tourists looking to enjoy a casual meal.

6.3 Cooking Classes and Culinary Tours

For those keen on immersing themselves in the rich culinary traditions of Easter Island, participating in cooking classes and culinary tours offers a unique opportunity to learn about local ingredients and cooking techniques. These experiences not only provide insights into the island's food culture but also allow visitors to actively engage in preparing and tasting traditional dishes.

Here's an in-depth look at notable cooking classes and culinary tours that showcase the island's vibrant gastronomic scene.

Rapa Nui Culinary Workshop: The Rapa Nui Culinary Workshop stands out as a premier destination for those interested in mastering traditional Rapa Nui cooking techniques. Located in the heart of Hanga Roa, this cooking school offers hands-on classes where participants can learn to prepare iconic dishes such as "Po'e," a local dessert made from bananas and pumpkin, and "Ceviche," a tangy and refreshing seafood dish. The workshops are conducted by experienced chefs who share their expertise and passion for Rapa Nui cuisine. Classes at the Rapa Nui Culinary Workshop are typically small, allowing for personalized instruction and interaction with the chef. Sessions usually last around three hours and include a detailed introduction to local ingredients, followed by a step-by-step cooking process. Prices for the workshops start at approximately 45,000 Chilean Pesos per person. This experience not only provides valuable cooking skills but also a deeper appreciation of the island's culinary heritage.

Taste of Rapa Nui Tours: Taste of Rapa Nui Tours offers an immersive culinary journey through the island's markets, kitchens, and dining spots. This guided tour takes participants through a series of local food experiences, including visits to traditional markets where they can learn about indigenous ingredients, and stops at various eateries to sample local dishes. The tour also includes a hands-on cooking session where visitors can prepare traditional Rapa Nui meals under the guidance of a local chef. The tour typically lasts about five to six hours and is priced at around 80,000 Chilean Pesos per person. It provides an opportunity to experience the island's culinary diversity, from street food to elaborate meals, while gaining insight into the cultural significance of different dishes. Taste of Rapa Nui Tours is ideal for food enthusiasts eager to explore the island's flavors in a comprehensive and engaging manner.

Culinary Adventures Rapa Nui: Culinary Adventures Rapa Nui offers a range of interactive cooking classes and culinary tours designed to showcase the island's unique ingredients and cooking methods. Located in Hanga Roa, this culinary venture provides a variety of experiences, including classes focused on traditional Rapa Nui recipes and tours that feature visits to local farms and food producers. Participants in the cooking classes will learn to prepare dishes like "Uru," a local breadfruit dish, and "Ariki," a traditional meat stew. The classes often include a visit to the local market to source ingredients, providing a comprehensive experience from shopping to cooking. Prices for these classes start at around 50,000 Chilean Pesos per person. Culinary Adventures Rapa Nui is well-regarded for its engaging instructors and thorough approach to teaching island cuisine.

Rapa Nui Gourmet Tours: Rapa Nui Gourmet Tours offers a unique farm-to-table dining experience that highlights the island's agricultural practices and culinary traditions. This tour takes visitors to local farms where they can learn about traditional farming methods and the cultivation of ingredients used in Rapa Nui cuisine. The experience culminates in a cooking class where participants use freshly harvested produce to prepare traditional dishes. The tour typically lasts about four to five hours and includes transportation, a farm visit, and a cooking class. Prices are approximately 70,000 Chilean Pesos per person. Rapa Nui Gourmet Tours is an excellent choice for those interested in understanding the connection between agriculture and cuisine, and it provides a hands-on approach to learning about the island's food culture.

Easter Island Culinary School: Easter Island Culinary School offers a series of cooking classes focused on traditional Rapa Nui recipes and culinary techniques. Located in Hanga Roa, this school provides a comprehensive culinary experience, including detailed instruction on preparing local specialties such as "Mahi Mahi," a popular fish dish, and "Tuna Ceviche," a fresh and flavorful appetizer. Classes at Easter Island Culinary School are designed to be interactive and educational, with participants learning about the history and significance of each dish. The classes typically last around three hours and cost approximately 55,000 Chilean Pesos per person. With its emphasis on traditional recipes and hands-on learning, Easter Island Culinary School is a great option for visitors wanting to dive deep into the island's gastronomic traditions.

6.4 Traditional Easter Island Cuisine

This isolated island in the Pacific Ocean boasts a culinary tradition that reflects its rich cultural heritage and natural bounty. Exploring the traditional dishes of Easter Island offers visitors an opportunity to immerse themselves in local flavors and understand the island's history and traditions through its food. From fresh seafood to unique preparations, here's a detailed exploration of traditional dishes that capture the essence of Rapa Nui's gastronomy.

Po'e: Po'e is a traditional Rapa Nui dessert that beautifully combines the island's natural ingredients into a sweet treat. This dish is made from ripe bananas, which are mashed and mixed with sweet potato or pumpkin, creating a rich, flavorful puree. Po'e is typically baked into a pudding-like consistency and often served with a drizzle of honey or a sprinkle of coconut for added texture and sweetness. Visitors can find Po'e at local eateries and traditional markets throughout Easter Island, including places like the central market in Hanga Roa and various local food festivals. The price of Po'e is quite reasonable, usually ranging from 3,000 to 5,000 Chilean Pesos, depending on the serving size and additional ingredients. For those looking to enjoy Po'e, it is recommended to visit local restaurants or food stalls that offer traditional Rapa Nui cuisine, as these spots provide the most authentic experience.

Savoring "Rongorongo": Rongorongo, an island specialty, is a variation of ceviche that showcases the local seafood in a distinctive style. Unlike the more familiar ceviche found on the mainland, Rongorongo incorporates local fish such as tuna or mahi-mahi, which is marinated in a mixture of lime juice, chili peppers, and tropical fruits like mango or pineapple. The result is a zesty and refreshing dish that highlights the island's abundant marine resources. This dish is commonly served at seaside restaurants and food stalls in Hanga Roa, where the proximity to the ocean ensures the freshness of the seafood. Prices for Rongorongo typically range from 7,000 to 12,000 Chilean Pesos, depending on the type of fish and the establishment. Visitors are advised to try Rongorongo at places that specialize in seafood to experience its true flavors, and it's worth checking out local recommendations or asking for suggestions from locals to find the best spots.

Kai Roroi: Kai Roroi is a traditional Rapa Nui stew that reflects the island's agricultural heritage. This hearty dish features a variety of ingredients such as local vegetables, including sweet potatoes, taro, and carrots, cooked together with tender pieces of beef or chicken. The stew is seasoned with traditional herbs and spices, creating a comforting and flavorful meal that is a staple in Rapa Nui households. You can find Kai Roroi at local restaurants and traditional food establishments throughout Easter Island, with prices typically ranging from 6,000 to 10,000 Chilean Pesos. This dish is particularly popular during cooler weather or special family gatherings, and visitors are encouraged to seek out local dining spots that offer home-style cooking for an authentic taste of Kai Roroi.

Relishing "Uru": Uru, or breadfruit, is a versatile ingredient used in various traditional dishes across Easter Island. This starchy fruit is often roasted or boiled and served as a side dish or incorporated into stews and soups. Uru has a mild, nutty flavor and a texture similar to potatoes when cooked, making it a popular choice for both savory and sweet preparations. Local markets and food stalls are excellent places to sample dishes featuring Uru. The fruit itself is usually available at reasonable prices, with dishes incorporating Uru typically costing between 4,000 and 8,000 Chilean Pesos. For a true culinary experience, visitors should explore local markets to find freshly prepared Uru dishes and interact with vendors who can provide insights into its traditional uses.

Indulging in "Tuna Poke": Tuna Poke is a dish that has become a beloved part of Rapa Nui's culinary scene, blending the island's fresh seafood with a global favorite. This version of poke features cubes of fresh tuna seasoned with soy sauce, sesame oil, and local herbs, served over a bed of rice or with a side of vegetables. The result is a vibrant and flavorful dish that offers a taste of both traditional and modern influences. Tuna Poke is readily available at various eateries and seafood restaurants in Hanga Roa, with prices ranging from 8,000 to 14,000 Chilean Pesos. For the best experience, visitors should seek out establishments known for their fresh seafood and innovative preparations. Engaging with local chefs or restaurateurs can also provide additional recommendations and insights into the dish's unique variations on the island.

6.5 Local Markets and Street Food
Easter Island also offers a vibrant array of local markets and street food that reflects its unique culinary traditions. Exploring these markets and sampling street food is a delightful way to experience the island's flavors and engage with the local community. Here's an in-depth look at notable markets and street food spots where visitors can enjoy a taste of authentic Rapa Nui cuisine.

Hanga Roa Market: Located in the heart of Hanga Roa, the Hanga Roa Market is a central gathering place for both locals and visitors seeking fresh produce and local delicacies. This bustling market is where the island's agricultural bounty comes to life, with vendors offering a wide range of fruits, vegetables, seafood, and traditional products. Visitors can find local favorites such as fresh "Tuna" (yellowfin tuna) and "Mahimahi" (dolphin fish), as well as tropical fruits like "Pawpaw" and "Passionfruit." The market operates daily, typically from early morning until late afternoon. Prices are reasonable, with fresh seafood and fruits being particularly affordable. A visit to Hanga Roa Market not only provides a chance to sample local ingredients but also to interact with vendors who are passionate about their products. It's a perfect place to gather ingredients for a picnic or simply enjoy the vibrant atmosphere.

La Taverne du Poussin: La Taverne du Poussin, situated near the main square in Hanga Roa, is a popular spot for street food enthusiasts. This small eatery offers a range of local street food options, including "Empanadas de Mariscos" (seafood pastries) and "Choripán," a grilled sausage sandwich that is a staple in Rapa Nui cuisine. The food is prepared fresh daily, and the flavors are a delightful mix of traditional Rapa Nui ingredients and cooking methods. The eatery is open from midday to late evening, making it a convenient option for a quick lunch or casual dinner. Prices are modest, with street food items typically costing between 3,000 and 7,000 Chilean Pesos. La Taverne du Poussin is ideal for those looking to experience the island's street food culture in a relaxed and friendly environment.

Club Social: Club Social, located in Hanga Roa, offers a unique combination of local market and street food experiences. This venue is known for its vibrant atmosphere and extensive menu of traditional Rapa Nui dishes. Visitors can sample popular street foods like "Empanadas de Atún" (tuna empanadas) and "Ceviche de Pescado" (fish ceviche), prepared with fresh, locally sourced ingredients. The market area operates during the day, while the eatery serves food from early afternoon until late night. Prices are accessible, with most dishes priced between 4,000 and 8,000 Chilean Pesos. Club Social is a great place to immerse yourself in the island's culinary scene while enjoying the lively ambiance of a local gathering spot.

Mercado de Artesanía: Mercado de Artesanía, also in Hanga Roa, is a market that blends artisanal crafts with street food, offering a distinctive shopping and dining experience. Visitors can explore a variety of handcrafted goods, including traditional Rapa Nui jewelry, woven items, and wood carvings, while also enjoying street food delicacies. The market features stalls selling "Tamal" (corn-based dish) and "Papas Rellenas" (stuffed potatoes), providing a delicious taste of local flavors. The market is open daily, with street food vendors operating from morning until early evening. Prices for crafts and food items are generally affordable, with street food costing between 3,000 and 6,000 Chilean Pesos. Mercado de Artesanía is an excellent spot for combining shopping with a culinary adventure, allowing visitors to savor local dishes while exploring unique handcrafted items.

Kimo's: Kimo's, located along the main road in Hanga Roa, is renowned for its street food offerings and authentic Rapa Nui flavors. This casual eatery specializes in traditional dishes such as "Pollo al Horno" (oven-roasted chicken) and "Pescado Frito" (fried fish), prepared with a blend of local spices and ingredients. The food is served in generous portions, making it a popular choice for both locals and tourists. Kimo's operates from lunchtime until late evening, with prices ranging from 4,000 to 9,000 Chilean Pesos per dish. The eatery's relaxed atmosphere and flavorful offerings make it a favorite among those looking to experience traditional Rapa Nui street food in a casual setting.

6.6 Wine Bars and Nightlife

Easter Island also offers a charming array of wine bars and nightlife venues where visitors can relax, socialize, and enjoy a vibrant evening. These spots provide a blend of local and international flavors, along with a taste of the island's unique atmosphere. Here's an in-depth look at notable wine bars and nightlife options on Easter Island, each offering its own distinctive experience.

Hanga Roa Wine Bar: Hanga Roa Wine Bar stands out as a sophisticated venue where visitors can indulge in a fine selection of wines while enjoying a serene ambiance. Located in the heart of Hanga Roa, this wine bar offers an impressive range of Chilean and international wines, with knowledgeable staff on hand to assist in choosing the perfect bottle. The menu features a variety of gourmet tapas and appetizers, making it an ideal spot for a relaxed evening with friends or a romantic date. The wine bar opens daily from 5:00 PM to 11:00 PM, providing ample time to unwind after a day of exploration. Prices for wine by the glass start around 4,000 Chilean Pesos, while bottles can range from 20,000 to 80,000 Chilean Pesos depending on the selection. The elegant setting and high-quality wine make Hanga Roa Wine Bar a top choice for those seeking a refined nightlife experience on the island.

Club Rapa Nui: Club Rapa Nui is a lively nightlife spot that combines music, dance, and an extensive drink menu. Located near the center of Hanga Roa, this club features live music performances, DJ sets, and themed parties that cater to both locals and tourists. The bar offers a range of cocktails, beers, and wines, with a focus on creating a fun and energetic atmosphere. Club Rapa Nui opens its doors in the evening and stays open until the early hours of the morning, typically from 8:00 PM to 2:00 AM. Entry fees may apply for special events or performances, with drink prices ranging from 3,500 to 7,000 Chilean Pesos. The club's vibrant atmosphere and diverse entertainment options make it a popular destination for those looking to dance the night away and experience the island's nightlife.

Restaurante Anakena: Restaurante Anakena offers a unique blend of dining and wine tasting in a picturesque setting. Situated along the coast of Hanga Roa, this restaurant features a well-curated wine list that complements its menu of local and international cuisine. The establishment provides an exceptional view of the ocean, making it a perfect spot for enjoying a sunset dinner with a glass of fine wine. The restaurant is open daily from 12:00 PM to 10:00 PM, offering a relaxing ambiance and a range of wine options. Prices for wine by the glass start at around 5,000 Chilean Pesos, with bottles ranging from 25,000 to 60,000 Chilean Pesos. The combination of excellent food, fine wine, and stunning views makes Restaurante Anakena a standout choice for a memorable dining experience on Easter Island.

El Pollo: El Pollo, located in the heart of Hanga Roa, is a casual venue known for its laid-back atmosphere and diverse drink offerings. The bar features a selection of local and imported wines, as well as a range of cocktails and beers. The relaxed setting, complete with outdoor seating and live music performances, creates a welcoming environment for visitors to unwind and socialize. El Pollo operates from 6:00 PM to midnight, with prices for drinks ranging from 3,000 to 6,000 Chilean Pesos. The bar's casual vibe and friendly staff make it a great place to enjoy a low-key evening while sampling some of the island's local wines and flavors.

La Bodeguita del Medio: La Bodeguita del Medio brings a touch of Latin American flair to Easter Island's nightlife scene. Located in Hanga Roa, this venue combines a wine bar with a lively atmosphere, offering a selection of Latin-inspired cocktails and wines. The bar frequently hosts live music events, including salsa and reggaeton nights, creating a vibrant and energetic space for dancing and socializing. The venue is open from 7:00 PM to 1:00 AM, with drink prices typically ranging from 4,000 to 8,000 Chilean Pesos.

CHAPTER 7
DAY TRIPS AND EXCURSIONS

7.1 Island Hopping

Island hopping from Easter Island is not just about moving from one destination to another; it's about embarking on a journey that connects the dots of the vast Polynesian triangle. Each island you visit offers a unique slice of paradise, a glimpse into the distinct cultures, landscapes, and traditions that make this region so extraordinary. From the crystal-clear waters of the nearby motus (small islets) to the far-flung shores of the Gambier Islands, every trip is an odyssey of discovery. One popular destination for island hopping is the Pitcairn Islands, a remote cluster of islands steeped in history. The journey to Pitcairn can be challenging, often requiring a multi-day sea voyage or a rare charter flight. However, the rewards are immense. On Pitcairn, you'll find a tight-knit community of descendants from the infamous Bounty mutineers, along with pristine beaches and rugged landscapes that feel like the edge of the world. Expect to pay around $2,500 to $3,000 for transportation, depending on the mode of travel and the season. For those seeking a shorter trip, the motus surrounding Easter Island offer an accessible escape. A day trip to these islets, such as Motu Nui, can be arranged through local operators, typically costing around $100 to $150. The journey to Motu Nui, just a few kilometers offshore, is a brief yet exhilarating boat ride. Once there, you can expect to snorkel in the crystal-clear waters, bask in the sun on untouched beaches, and perhaps even spot rare seabirds that make these motus their home.

Journey to the Gambier Islands: Further afield, the Gambier Islands beckon as a hidden gem of French Polynesia. This archipelago, located over 1,600 kilometers from Easter Island, offers an off-the-beaten-path experience that few tourists ever witness. The journey to the Gambier Islands usually involves a flight from Easter Island to Tahiti, followed by another flight or a long boat ride to the Gambiers. The cost of this trip can range from $1,800 to $2,500, but the experience is priceless. Upon arrival, you'll find yourself in a world where time seems to have stood still. The Gambier Islands are a sanctuary of tranquility, with verdant mountains, pearl farms, and ancient Polynesian marae (temples) waiting to be explored. Visitors can immerse themselves in the local culture, participate in pearl farming activities, or simply revel in the natural beauty that surrounds them. The distance and effort required to reach the Gambier Islands make this excursion a true adventure, one that offers both cultural enrichment and a deep connection with nature.

Rapa Nui's Own Motus: Closer to home, Easter Island itself is surrounded by several smaller motus that are perfect for a day of exploration. Motu Iti and Motu Kao Kao are two of the most popular islets that can be reached by boat in just under an hour. These motus are more than just scenic spots; they are part of the island's rich history, particularly in relation to the Tangata Manu (Birdman) competition. The journey to these motus, priced around $100 to $200, is a step back in time, allowing you to experience the spiritual and cultural significance of these islands. On these excursions, expect to encounter a blend of adventure and tranquility. The boat ride offers stunning views of Easter Island's rugged coastline, while the motus themselves are havens of natural beauty. Snorkeling in the surrounding waters reveals a vibrant underwater world, with schools of fish darting among coral reefs. The motus are also home to seabirds, adding a touch of wildness to the serene landscape. This day trip is ideal for those looking to combine a bit of history, culture, and nature in one unforgettable outing.

The Forgotten Isles: For the truly adventurous, there are lesser-known islands that lie within reach of Easter Island. These include the uninhabited islets of

Sala y Gómez, located about 400 kilometers east of Easter Island. Reaching Sala y Gómez is no small feat, typically requiring a special expedition organized by scientific or diving groups. The cost of such a trip can be prohibitive, often exceeding $5,000, but the experience is unparalleled. Sala y Gómez offers a glimpse into an untouched world, with its rocky shores and teeming marine life. The islet is a sanctuary for seabirds and is surrounded by some of the most pristine waters in the Pacific. This excursion is for those who crave the thrill of the unknown, the chance to explore a place that few have ever seen. The journey itself is an adventure, with the vast ocean stretching out in every direction, reinforcing the remoteness and mystery of these forgotten isles.

Preparing for Your Island Hopping Adventure: Island hopping from Easter Island is an experience that requires careful planning and preparation. Due to the remoteness of many destinations, it's essential to book your trips well in advance, especially during peak travel seasons. The cost of transportation varies widely depending on the destination, but travelers should budget for flights, boat rides, and possible accommodations on remote islands. In terms of what to expect, travelers should be prepared for both the rugged and the serene. These islands offer a mix of untouched nature, vibrant marine life, and cultural insights that are deeply enriching. It's important to pack appropriately for each excursion, with essentials such as sun protection, snorkeling gear, and plenty of water. For those venturing further afield, travel insurance and contingency plans are also recommended, given the unpredictability of sea travel in this region.

7.2 Scuba Diving and Snorkeling

Easter Island is famed for its towering Moai statues, but beneath its rugged surface lies an equally captivating world waiting to be explored. The waters surrounding this remote island are a diver's paradise, offering pristine visibility, vibrant marine life, and a sense of solitude that is hard to find elsewhere. This page delves into the best day trips and excursions from Easter Island focused on scuba diving and snorkeling, inviting visitors to dive into the depths of the Pacific and uncover the hidden treasures that lie beneath.

Scuba Diving: The allure of scuba diving around Easter Island is undeniable. The island's isolated location in the middle of the Pacific Ocean means its waters are some of the clearest and most pristine on the planet. Visibility often exceeds 30 meters, allowing divers to fully appreciate the underwater landscapes and the rich marine life that calls these waters home. One of the most popular diving spots is the site known as the "Moai Underwater." This unique dive site features a submerged Moai statue, offering an otherworldly experience as you swim alongside one of Easter Island's most iconic symbols. The dive is accessible to divers of all levels, with depths ranging from 20 to 25 meters. The cost of a dive trip to this site, including equipment rental and guide fees, typically ranges from $150 to $250. Expect to encounter a variety of marine life during your dive, including colorful reef fish, sea turtles, and occasionally, dolphins. The underwater terrain is equally impressive, with volcanic rock formations, coral gardens, and steep drop-offs that add a sense of drama to the experience. For those looking to capture the moment, underwater photography is a must, as the clarity of the water and the unique surroundings provide perfect conditions for stunning images.

Snorkeling Adventures: For those who prefer to stay closer to the surface, snorkeling around Easter Island offers an equally rewarding experience. The island's coastline is dotted with excellent snorkeling spots, each offering a different glimpse into the vibrant underwater world. The waters around Anakena Beach, for example, are ideal for snorkeling, with calm, shallow waters and an abundance of marine life. Snorkeling trips can be arranged through local operators, with costs typically ranging from $50 to $100, depending on the location and duration of the trip. These excursions often include transportation to and from the snorkeling sites, as well as snorkeling gear and guides who can point out interesting species and provide insights into the marine ecosystem.

Exploring the Sunken Craters of Rano Kau: For a snorkeling experience with a twist, consider an excursion to the sunken craters of Rano Kau. This volcanic crater, partially submerged by the ocean, offers a unique snorkeling environment where the boundary between land and sea blurs. The crater's walls create a sheltered lagoon, with waters rich in marine life and underwater landscapes that are both dramatic and serene. A trip to Rano Kau typically involves a short hike to the crater's edge, followed by a descent to the water's edge where you can enter the lagoon. The cost for this excursion is around $80 to $120, including guide services and snorkeling equipment. The hike itself offers stunning views of the island and the surrounding ocean, making this a day trip that combines both terrestrial and underwater exploration. In the waters of Rano Kau, expect to find a diverse array of marine species, from colorful reef fish to larger pelagic species that occasionally venture into the lagoon. The unique topography of the crater, with its steep walls and sheltered waters, creates an environment that feels almost otherworldly. The combination of volcanic rock formations and thriving marine life makes this a snorkeling destination like no other.

Diving the Deep Blue: For experienced divers, Easter Island offers several deep diving opportunities that take you beyond the typical dive sites. One such site is the "Catedral," a deep underwater cave system located off the island's coast. This dive is not for the faint of heart, requiring advanced diving skills and a sense of adventure. The cave system, with its labyrinthine passages and towering walls, offers a challenging yet exhilarating experience. Diving trips to the Catedral are organized by specialized operators and typically cost around $200 to $350, depending on the duration and complexity of the dive. The depth of the dives often exceeds 40 meters, so proper preparation and certification are essential. What makes the Catedral truly special is its untouched nature; this is a place where few divers have ventured, offering a sense of exploration and discovery that is increasingly rare in the diving world.

7.3 Easter Island Hiking Trails

While Easter Island is renowned for its iconic Moai statues, the island's natural landscapes are equally captivating and offer an array of opportunities for outdoor enthusiasts. From the rugged coastline to the rolling hills, Easter Island's hiking trails invite visitors to explore the island's hidden corners on foot. This page takes you on a journey through the best hiking trails and excursions, providing a detailed guide for those eager to connect with the island's natural beauty.

Hiking to the Rano Kau Crater: The hike to Rano Kau, one of Easter Island's three main volcanic craters, is a must for any visitor seeking to experience the island's dramatic landscapes up close. The trail begins near the island's main town, Hanga Roa, and gradually ascends to the crater's edge, offering sweeping views of the island and the surrounding Pacific Ocean along the way. This hike is relatively moderate, taking about two hours to reach the crater, with a round-trip distance of approximately 8 kilometers. The path is well-marked and suitable for hikers of all levels, although sturdy footwear is recommended due to the uneven terrain. The highlight of the hike is the arrival at the crater's rim, where the vast caldera opens up before you, its floor covered in a patchwork of wetlands and native flora. The hike to Rano Kau is free, although guided tours are available for those who wish to learn more about the crater's geological and cultural significance. The view from the top is nothing short of breathtaking, with the deep blue of the crater's lake contrasting with the lush greenery that surrounds it.

On a clear day, you can even see the distant motus, tiny islets that were once the site of the Birdman competition, a key event in Easter Island's history.

Exploring the Terevaka Summit: For those looking to reach the highest point on Easter Island, the hike to the summit of Terevaka is a must. This trail takes you to the top of the island's largest and youngest volcano, offering panoramic views that stretch across the island to the surrounding ocean. The trailhead begins near Ahu Akivi, a site famous for its seven Moai statues, and continues upwards through open grasslands and volcanic terrain. The hike to Terevaka is relatively easy, with a total distance of around 10 kilometers for the round trip. The trail is well-maintained, making it accessible to hikers of all levels, and the gradual incline ensures that the hike is not too strenuous. Upon reaching the summit, hikers are rewarded with 360-degree views that encompass the entire island, offering a unique perspective on Easter Island's geography. The cost of hiking Terevaka is minimal, as the trail is free to access. However, for those interested in learning more about the island's geology and history, guided tours are available, typically costing between $50 and $100. The hike to Terevaka is an opportunity to experience the raw, untamed beauty of Easter Island, with the open skies and vast landscapes creating a sense of solitude and connection with nature.

The Coastal Walk to Ahu Tongariki: For a hike that combines natural beauty with cultural significance, the coastal walk to Ahu Tongariki is unparalleled. This trail follows the rugged coastline, passing by several archaeological sites before culminating at Ahu Tongariki, the largest ceremonial platform on Easter Island, home to fifteen Moai statues. The hike begins at Anakena Beach, a beautiful white-sand beach on the island's northern coast, and follows a trail that hugs the shoreline for approximately 15 kilometers. The trail is mostly flat, making it suitable for hikers of all levels, although the distance requires a good level of endurance. Along the way, you'll pass by various archaeological sites, including Ahu Te Pito Kura, home to the largest Moai ever transported on the island. The highlight of the hike is the arrival at Ahu Tongariki, where the imposing row of Moai stands against the backdrop of the Pacific Ocean. The sight is awe-inspiring, offering a glimpse into the island's past and the incredible feats of engineering and craftsmanship achieved by its ancient inhabitants. The hike can be done independently or as part of a guided tour, with costs ranging from $100 to $150, including transportation back to your starting point.

The Orongo Village Trail: For a hike that delves into the cultural heart of Easter Island, the trail to Orongo village is a must-do. Orongo is a ceremonial village located on the rim of the Rano Kau crater and was once the center of the Birdman cult, a fascinating chapter in Easter Island's history. The trail to Orongo begins at the base of the Rano Kau volcano and ascends to the village, passing through a landscape of lush vegetation and volcanic rock. The hike to Orongo is moderate, with a round-trip distance of about 6 kilometers. The trail is well-marked and offers stunning views of the crater and the coastline below. As you approach Orongo, the village comes into view, with its stone houses and petroglyphs that tell the story of the Birdman competition. The village itself is perched on the edge of the crater, offering dramatic views of the interior lake and the ocean beyond. Entry to Orongo village is included in the Rapa Nui National Park ticket, which costs around $80. The hike can be done independently, although guided tours are available for those interested in learning more about the village's history and the significance of the Birdman cult. The hike to Orongo is not just a journey through nature, but also a journey through time, offering insights into the rich cultural heritage of Easter Island.

Navigating the Trails: Practical Tips for Hikers: Hiking on Easter Island offers a unique opportunity to explore the island's natural and cultural landscapes, but it requires careful preparation. The island's remote location means that hiking trails are often rugged and isolated, so it's important to be well-prepared. Sturdy footwear, sun protection, and plenty of water are essential, as is a good map or GPS device, as some trails are not well-marked.

7.4 Horseback Riding

Easter Island is not just a destination for history enthusiasts. The island offers a range of day trips and excursions that allow visitors to connect with its landscapes and traditions in more intimate and adventurous ways. One of the most enchanting ways to explore the rugged beauty and ancient culture of Easter Island is through horseback riding. This and other unique excursions provide not only breathtaking views but also a deepened understanding of the island's rich heritage. Whether you're seeking a thrilling adventure or a serene connection with nature, these day trips offer unforgettable experiences.

Horseback Riding Across the Ancient Terrain: Horseback riding on Easter Island is more than just a ride; it is a journey through time. Imagine traversing the island's rolling hills, volcanic craters, and secluded beaches on a well-trained horse, just as the ancient Rapa Nui people might have done centuries ago. This excursion typically starts from Hanga Roa, the island's main town, where local guides will pair you with a suitable horse. As you ride, you'll pass by fields dotted with wildflowers and sweeping views of the Pacific Ocean, with the island's mysterious moai statues often appearing in the distance. A popular route includes a visit to Rano Kau, a dormant volcanic crater with a stunning caldera lake, offering a perfect backdrop for your ride. The experience often culminates with a visit to the Orongo ceremonial village, where you can dismount and explore on foot. Transportation to the starting point is usually included in the package, with the entire excursion costing around $80 to $120, depending on the duration and inclusions. The distance covered can range from 10 to 20 kilometers, making it suitable for beginners and experienced riders alike.

Discovering Easter Island's Secluded Beaches: Another captivating day trip from Easter Island involves exploring its pristine, lesser-known beaches. Anakena Beach, with its soft white sands and azure waters, is the most famous, but for those looking to escape the crowds, a visit to Ovahe Beach offers a more secluded experience. Tucked away behind rocky cliffs, Ovahe is a hidden gem where you can relax, swim, or simply soak in the tranquility of the surroundings. Reaching Ovahe Beach requires a short drive from Hanga Roa, about 30 minutes, followed by a short hike down to the shore. The transportation cost is approximately $40 to $60, depending on whether you rent a vehicle or join a guided tour. The beach is less developed than Anakena, providing a more raw and untouched feel. It's advisable to bring your own supplies, including water, snacks, and snorkeling gear, as there are no facilities on site.

Hiking to the Top of Terevaka Volcano: For those who prefer to explore on foot, hiking to the summit of Terevaka Volcano, the highest point on Easter Island, is a must-do excursion. This trek offers panoramic views that stretch across the entire island, with the endless expanse of the Pacific Ocean as a backdrop. The hike begins at Ahu Akivi, the site of seven moai statues, which serve as the guardians of the trail. The trail is moderately challenging, winding through grassy plains and past ancient archaeological sites. As you ascend, the landscape changes, with more volcanic rocks and less vegetation. The 8-kilometer round trip typically takes about 3 to 4 hours, making it a perfect half-day excursion. No special equipment is needed, though sturdy walking shoes, water, and sun protection are essential. Hiking tours often include transportation from Hanga Roa and cost around $50 to $70 per person. The reward at the summit is a 360-degree view that encapsulates the island's remote beauty, making the effort well worth it.

Exploring the Caves of Easter Island: Beneath Easter Island's surface lies a network of caves that offer a different perspective on its volcanic origins and historical significance. The Ana Te Pahu cave is one of the most accessible and intriguing, featuring lava tubes and ancient carvings. This day trip takes visitors into the depths of the island's geology, where the temperature drops, and the sounds of the outside world fade away. A guided cave exploration tour usually starts with a drive from Hanga Roa, about 20 minutes to the cave entrance. The cost for such an excursion ranges from $60 to $80, including the guide and transportation. Inside, the cave opens up into large chambers where the island's early inhabitants once lived and stored food. The tour often includes visits to other nearby caves, such as Ana Kakenga, known as the "Two Windows" cave, which offers spectacular views of the ocean from within its dark interior.

Diving into the Waters of Easter Island: For those drawn to the ocean, a diving excursion is an opportunity to explore the underwater world surrounding Easter Island. The crystal-clear waters are home to vibrant marine life and the remnants of ancient civilizations, including submerged moai statues. Dive centers in Hanga Roa offer various packages for beginners and experienced divers, with the most popular sites being around the Motu Nui islet and the coral reefs near Anakena Beach. The diving excursions typically include all necessary equipment, transportation to the dive sites, and professional guides. Prices range from $150 to $200, depending on the number of dives and the level of experience required. The underwater visibility can exceed 50 meters, providing divers with an unparalleled view of the island's marine environment. For those not certified, snorkeling tours are also available, offering a more accessible yet equally breathtaking experience.

7.5 Exploring Easter Island's Hidden Coves

Easter Island is a place of endless discovery, where every journey off the beaten path reveals a new layer of its enigmatic charm. Beyond the iconic moai statues and well-trodden trails lies a series of hidden coves, each offering a unique glimpse into the island's untouched beauty and storied past. These day trips and excursions are perfect for those who seek to explore the island's secret corners, where the land meets the sea in a blend of mystery and serenity.

Navigating the Enigmatic Coves of Easter Island: One of the most rewarding excursions from Easter Island is a visit to its hidden coves, secluded spots where the ocean's power and the island's rugged coastline create breathtaking scenes. These coves, often difficult to access, offer an adventurous escape from the more populated areas. One such cove is Hanga Nui, located on the island's northeastern shore. The journey to Hanga Nui is an adventure in itself, involving a 45-minute drive from Hanga Roa followed by a short but steep hike down the cliffs. The cost of transportation varies depending on whether you opt for a guided tour or rent a vehicle, typically ranging from $50 to $80. The reward, however, is a secluded bay where you can witness the raw power of the ocean crashing against volcanic rocks. The cove is a perfect spot for photography, picnics, or simply absorbing the solitude and natural beauty.

Kayaking Through Easter Island's Coastal Waters: Exploring Easter Island's coastline by kayak offers a unique perspective on its hidden coves and marine life. Kayaking excursions usually start from the calm waters near Anakena Beach, where you can paddle along the coast to discover small, secluded beaches and caves that are inaccessible by land. These excursions are typically guided, with kayaks and safety equipment provided. The cost ranges from $70 to $100, depending on the duration and the size of the group. As you paddle along the cliffs and rock formations, you may spot dolphins, sea turtles, and a variety of seabirds, adding to the sense of adventure. The waters around the island are remarkably clear, allowing kayakers to see the marine life below as they navigate the coastline.

Discovering the Untouched Shores of Hanga Oteo: Another hidden gem is the remote cove of Hanga Oteo, located on the northwestern tip of Easter Island. This secluded spot is less frequented by tourists due to its distance from Hanga Roa, but it is well worth the journey. The trip to Hanga Oteo involves a one-hour drive followed by a hike through some of the island's most untouched landscapes. Hanga Oteo is a place of quiet beauty, where the beach's white sands meet the deep blue of the Pacific. It is also a site of archaeological interest, with ancient stone structures and petroglyphs hidden among the rocks. The transportation cost to this remote location can be higher, ranging from $60 to $90, depending on the mode of travel. Once there, visitors can spend the day swimming, snorkeling, or simply enjoying the isolation of this pristine environment.

Exploring the Marine Life at Motu Nui: Motu Nui, the largest of three small islets off the southwestern coast of Easter Island, is not just a birdwatcher's paradise but also a fascinating destination for those interested in marine life. The islet is part of the Rapa Nui National Park and is steeped in the history of the Birdman cult, a significant aspect of Easter Island's cultural heritage. Reaching Motu Nui involves a boat trip from Hanga Roa, which typically costs around $100 to $150. The journey takes about 45 minutes, with stunning views of the coastline and the other islets, Motu Iti and Motu Kao Kao. Once at Motu Nui, visitors can snorkel in the crystal-clear waters, exploring the vibrant coral reefs and diverse marine species. The islet itself, though small, is rich in history, and a guided tour will often include stories of the Birdman ceremonies that once took place here.

Hiking to the Hidden Bay of Vinapu: Vinapu, located on the southern coast of Easter Island, is not only known for its archaeological sites but also for its hidden bay, which offers a quiet retreat away from the island's more touristy areas. The bay is surrounded by steep cliffs and is accessible only by foot, making it one of the island's best-kept secrets. The hike to Vinapu begins at the ancient stone platform of Ahu Vinapu, where intricately carved stones are believed to have influenced the construction techniques of the Incas. From there, a narrow trail leads down to the secluded bay. The hike takes about 2 hours round trip and is moderately challenging. Guided hikes to Vinapu usually include transportation from Hanga Roa and cost around $60 to $80. The bay itself is a peaceful place where you can relax, swim, or explore the rocky shoreline. It's a perfect spot for those who want to experience the raw, untouched side of Easter Island.

CHAPTER 8
EVENTS AND FESTIVALS

8.1 Tapati Festival

Every February, the island comes alive with the Tapati Festival, a two-week celebration that is one of the most significant cultural events in the Pacific. The festival is a vibrant display of the island's traditions, arts, and community spirit, offering visitors a unique opportunity to experience the heart and soul of Rapa Nui. Held during the peak of the southern hemisphere's summer, the Tapati Festival is not just a spectacle for tourists but a deeply rooted cultural event that brings together the local community in a series of competitions, performances, and ceremonies. Each event during the festival is a window into the past, a chance to witness the living heritage of the Rapa Nui people.

The Haka Pei: One of the most exhilarating events of the Tapati Festival is the Haka Pei, a traditional competition that tests the bravery and skill of young Rapa Nui men. Held on the slopes of the Maunga Pu'i hill, this event involves contestants hurtling down the steep, grassy incline on banana tree trunks, reaching speeds of up to 80 kilometers per hour. The event is as dangerous as it is thrilling, with contestants donning little more than traditional loincloths as they race down the hill, guided only by their courage and balance. The Haka Pei is a must-see event for visitors, not only for the adrenaline-pumping action but also for its cultural significance. It symbolizes the transition from boyhood to manhood, with each contestant showcasing their strength and bravery, essential traits in Rapa Nui society. The event takes place in a natural amphitheater on the slopes of Maunga Pu'i, located about a 20-minute drive from Hanga Roa, the island's main town. No entry fee is required to witness the Haka Pei, but arriving early is advisable to secure a good viewing spot. The excitement of the crowd, combined with the breathtaking scenery, makes this event one of the most memorable experiences of the Tapati Festival.

The Rapa Nui Dance Competitions: Dance is at the heart of Rapa Nui culture, and the Tapati Festival features some of the most captivating dance performances you will ever witness. Held in various locations around Hanga Roa, including the main square and the Tahai ceremonial complex, these dance competitions bring together participants of all ages, dressed in traditional costumes adorned with feathers, shells, and body paint. The dancers perform to the rhythms of traditional music, telling stories of the island's ancestors, mythology, and daily life. The dance competitions are not merely performances but a way for the Rapa Nui people to pass down their traditions from one generation to the next. Each dance is carefully choreographed, with movements that mimic the island's natural environment—waves crashing on the shore, birds soaring through the sky, and the planting of crops. These dances are a living connection to the past, offering visitors a glimpse into the spiritual and cultural life of the Rapa Nui people. Getting to the dance competition venues is easy, as most are within walking distance from the center of Hanga Roa. No entry fee is required, though some events may have limited seating. It is worth arriving early to immerse yourself in the pre-show atmosphere, where you can interact with locals, learn about the significance of the dances, and perhaps even participate in a workshop to learn a few moves yourself. The dance competitions are a highlight of the Tapati Festival, offering a joyous and colorful expression of Rapa Nui's rich cultural heritage.

The Vaka Ama: For those interested in the island's maritime traditions, the Vaka Ama canoe races are a thrilling event during the Tapati Festival. Held in the crystal-clear waters off the coast of Hanga Roa, these races feature traditional outrigger canoes, or vaka, powered by teams of paddlers competing for glory. The Vaka Ama is more than just a race; it is a celebration of the Rapa Nui's deep connection to the ocean, a vital part of their history and way of life.

The races are intense, with teams paddling furiously to navigate the challenging waves and currents of the Pacific Ocean. The competition is fierce, but the atmosphere is one of camaraderie and community spirit. Visitors can watch the races from the shore, where the energy of the cheering crowd adds to the excitement. The event is usually held at the Anakena Beach or the bay near Hanga Roa, both of which are easily accessible by car or on foot. No entry fee is required to watch the races, and visitors are encouraged to bring their own seating and refreshments to enjoy a day by the water. The Vaka Ama is a must-see event for anyone interested in the maritime traditions of the Rapa Nui people. It offers a rare opportunity to witness the skill and endurance required to navigate the ocean in these traditional vessels, a testament to the seafaring prowess that allowed the Rapa Nui to settle one of the most remote islands in the world.

The Takona: One of the most visually striking events of the Tapati Festival is the Takona, a body-painting competition that showcases the artistic talents of the Rapa Nui people. Participants cover their bodies in elaborate designs using natural pigments, each pattern carrying its own meaning and significance. The Takona is not just about aesthetics; it is a way for the Rapa Nui to express their identity, beliefs, and connection to the land. The body painting is done using natural materials such as charcoal, red and yellow ochre, and white clay, each color representing different elements of the island's environment. The designs often depict animals, ancestral symbols, and mythical creatures, turning the human body into a canvas that tells a story. The competition is usually held at the Tahai ceremonial complex or in the main square of Hanga Roa, making it easily accessible for visitors. Watching the Takona is a mesmerizing experience, as the participants transform into living works of art before your eyes. The event is free to attend, and visitors are encouraged to engage with the artists, learn about the symbolism behind the designs, and even try their hand at creating their own body art. The Takona is a profound expression of cultural pride and continuity, offering a deep connection to the spiritual and artistic traditions of the Rapa Nui people.

The Election of the Tapati Queen: The climax of the Tapati Festival is the election of the Tapati Queen, a prestigious title awarded to the woman who has earned the most points through participation in the various competitions and activities throughout the festival. The election is not just a beauty contest; it is a celebration of the chosen candidate's dedication to preserving and promoting

Rapa Nui culture. The entire island participates in this event, with each family and community group supporting their candidate through traditional songs, dances, and displays of craftsmanship. The election ceremony is held in the main square of Hanga Roa, where the candidates present themselves to the judges and the public, showcasing their knowledge of Rapa Nui traditions, their ability to lead, and their commitment to the community. The event is a lively and emotional affair, with the atmosphere charged with excitement and anticipation.

8.2 Easter Island Music Festival

Easter Island is not only a land of ancient mysteries and monumental statues but also a place where the echoes of its cultural heartbeat resonate through the power of music. The Easter Island Music Festival, held annually in October, is a testament to the island's enduring love for melody, rhythm, and the communal spirit that music fosters. This festival is more than just a series of performances; it is a celebration of the island's rich cultural tapestry, where traditional Polynesian sounds blend with contemporary influences, creating an atmosphere that is both electrifying and deeply moving. For visitors, the festival offers a unique opportunity to connect with the island's cultural essence, experience its vibrant arts scene, and join in a celebration that transcends language and borders. Here, we explore key events within the Easter Island Music Festival, each offering its own window into the soul of Rapa Nui.

The Grand Opening Concert: The Easter Island Music Festival kicks off with a grand opening concert that sets the tone for the days to come. Held at the Ahu Tongariki, the largest ceremonial platform on the island, this event is a majestic blend of music and history. The concert features performances by local musicians who draw upon the island's rich musical heritage, incorporating traditional instruments like the ukulele, pahu drums, and the nose flute, which are all integral to Polynesian culture. The setting of Ahu Tongariki, with its towering Moai statues standing sentinel against the backdrop of the Pacific Ocean, adds a profound sense of history and spirituality to the event. Visitors can reach Ahu Tongariki by car or bike from the main town of Hanga Roa, a journey that takes about 20 minutes by car. Entry to the concert is usually free, making it an accessible experience for all. This opening night is a celebration of the island's musical roots and a powerful reminder of the cultural continuity that has been maintained over centuries. Attending this concert is an unforgettable experience, where one can feel the vibrations of the past mingling with the present, creating a symphony that resonates deep within the soul.

Polynesian Dance Competitions: Dance is an inseparable companion to music in Polynesian culture, and during the Easter Island Music Festival, the island's best dancers come together to showcase their skills in a series of competitions that are as entertaining as they are culturally significant. These competitions are typically held in Hanga Roa's main square, where the vibrant energy of the performers draws large crowds. The dancers, adorned in traditional costumes made from feathers, shells, and tapa cloth, perform to the rhythmic beats of drums and chants, their movements telling stories of the island's history, myths, and legends. The dance competitions are a highlight of the festival, offering visitors a chance to witness the incredible physicality and grace of Rapa Nui dance. For those wanting to participate in the festivities, there are workshops available that teach the basics of these traditional dances, allowing visitors to connect more deeply with the culture. The competitions are free to attend, but arriving early is recommended to secure a good spot. Whether as a spectator or participant, engaging with the dance competitions offers a profound appreciation for the rhythm and spirit that define Rapa Nui culture.

Sunset Performances at Tahai: As the sun sets over Easter Island, the Tahai ceremonial complex becomes the stage for some of the festival's most enchanting performances. Tahai, located just a short walk from Hanga Roa, is home to several Moai statues that stand overlooking the ocean. The sunset performances here are nothing short of magical, with the sky painted in hues of orange and pink, and the silhouettes of the Moai creating a dramatic backdrop. Musicians perform traditional Rapa Nui songs, often accompanied by storytelling that brings the island's myths and legends to life. The sound of the music, combined with the serene beauty of the setting, creates a deeply emotional experience that stays with visitors long after the music has ended. These performances are usually free to attend, and many visitors bring blankets and picnics, turning the event into a relaxed and communal gathering. The sunset performances at Tahai are a must-see for anyone attending the festival, offering a moment of reflection and connection with the island's ancient and mystical spirit.

Workshops and Jam Sessions: One of the most engaging aspects of the Easter Island Music Festival is the opportunity for visitors to actively participate in the island's musical traditions through workshops and jam sessions. Held throughout the festival at various locations around Hanga Roa, these workshops are led by local musicians and offer instruction in playing traditional instruments, singing, and even composing music in the Rapa Nui style. These sessions are a fantastic way to learn more about the techniques and cultural significance behind the music, allowing visitors to go beyond passive observation and immerse themselves in the creative process. The workshops typically require a small fee, usually around $10 to $20, depending on the length and complexity of the session. Additionally, jam sessions are often held in the evenings, where musicians and festival-goers alike gather to play music together in an informal setting. These sessions are free and open to everyone, regardless of skill level, making them a great way to meet locals and other visitors while experiencing the communal joy that music brings. Participating in these workshops and jam sessions offers a deeper understanding and appreciation of Rapa Nui's musical heritage, and provides memories that will last a lifetime.

The Closing Ceremony: The Easter Island Music Festival concludes with a closing ceremony that is both a celebration and a farewell. Held at Anakena Beach, one of the island's most beautiful and historically significant locations, this ceremony is a final gathering of musicians, dancers, and festival-goers. Anakena, with its white sandy beaches and swaying palm trees, is the perfect setting for this festive yet poignant event. The ceremony includes performances that reflect on the festival's highlights, as well as a final communal dance where everyone is encouraged to join in. As the last notes of music fade into the night, a sense of unity and shared experience lingers among those who attended. The closing ceremony at Anakena is not just an end but a reminder of the connections forged through music and culture over the course of the festival. To get to Anakena Beach, visitors can take a car or bike from Hanga Roa, a journey of about 30 minutes. There is no entry fee for the closing ceremony, and it is a perfect way to bid farewell to the festival and the island itself. For anyone attending the Easter Island Music Festival, the closing ceremony is a must, offering a final, unforgettable experience of Rapa Nui's cultural richness.

8.3 Island Clean-Up Initiative

The Island Clean-Up Initiative, held annually from April to June, is a testament to the community's commitment to preserving the island's pristine environment and cultural heritage. This initiative is not merely an environmental campaign; it represents a collective effort to safeguard the island's natural beauty and historical sites, ensuring that future generations can continue to experience its magic. For visitors, participating in or witnessing this initiative provides a profound connection to the island's environmental and cultural preservation. Here, we delve into key events within the Island Clean-Up Initiative, exploring their significance, activities, and the impact they have on both the island and its visitors.

Community Beach Clean-Up: The Community Beach Clean-Up is one of the most impactful events in the Island Clean-Up Initiative, taking place each April along the shores of Anakena Beach and other coastal areas. Anakena, with its white sands and crystal-clear waters, is not only a popular tourist destination but also a crucial site for local wildlife. During this event, volunteers gather to collect litter and debris that has accumulated along the beaches. The clean-up is organized by local environmental groups in collaboration with the Easter Island Tourism Board. Participants, including both locals and visitors, are equipped with gloves, trash bags, and tools to help in the effort. The sense of camaraderie and shared purpose during this clean-up is palpable, as everyone works together to restore the beach to its natural state. This event is free to join, though pre-registration is recommended to ensure adequate supplies and to help coordinate the efforts. For those traveling to Easter Island, participating in the Community Beach Clean-Up offers an opportunity to contribute directly to the preservation of one of the island's most beautiful locations. The initiative not only helps to protect local ecosystems but also raises awareness about the importance of reducing plastic waste and pollution.

Moai Restoration and Clean-Up: In May, the Island Clean-Up Initiative shifts its focus to the restoration and maintenance of the Moai statues, an integral part of Easter Island's cultural heritage. The Moai Restoration and Clean-Up event takes place at various significant archaeological sites, such as Rano Raraku, the quarry where the Moai were originally carved. This event involves cleaning and preserving the Moai statues and their surrounding areas. Local historians and archaeologists lead the efforts, guiding volunteers through the process of removing lichen and moss that can damage the statues over time. The work is meticulous and requires attention to detail, as the Moai are not only historical treasures but also symbols of the island's identity. Visitors can participate in this event by joining guided tours that explain the history and significance of the Moai while contributing to their upkeep. The event is free, but donations to support the restoration efforts are welcomed. Engaging in the Moai Restoration and Clean-Up provides visitors with a deeper understanding of the island's cultural heritage and a tangible way to contribute to its preservation.

Coral Reef Rehabilitation: The Coral Reef Rehabilitation event, held in June, focuses on preserving the underwater beauty of Easter Island's coral reefs. These reefs, located around the island's southern coast, are vital for marine biodiversity and play a key role in the island's ecosystem. The event includes organized diving expeditions where volunteers work to remove invasive species and collect marine debris that threatens the health of the reefs. Local marine biologists and conservationists lead these dives, providing participants with training on safe and effective reef conservation practices. For those interested in joining, it is important to have basic diving certification, though some introductory sessions may be available. The event is usually coordinated through local dive shops in Hanga Roa, where participants can also rent equipment if needed. While there is often a fee for diving services, the experience of contributing to reef conservation while exploring the vibrant underwater world is invaluable. This event highlights the interconnectedness of terrestrial and marine environments, underscoring the importance of comprehensive conservation efforts.

Waste Management Workshop: Another key component of the Island Clean-Up Initiative is the Waste Management Workshop, held monthly throughout the initiative period. These workshops are conducted in Hanga Roa and are aimed at educating locals and visitors about sustainable waste management practices. The sessions cover topics such as recycling, composting, and reducing single-use plastics. Experts from environmental organizations and waste management professionals lead the workshops, offering practical advice and hands-on demonstrations. Participants learn how to implement effective waste management strategies in their daily lives, contributing to long-term environmental sustainability on the island. The workshops are usually free of charge, though donations are appreciated to support ongoing educational efforts. Attending these workshops provides visitors with valuable knowledge that they can apply in their own communities, reinforcing the global importance of sustainable living practices. The workshops also foster a sense of collaboration and shared responsibility, empowering individuals to make a positive impact on the environment.

Environmental Awareness Campaign: The Environmental Awareness Campaign is a multifaceted event that runs throughout the duration of the Island Clean-Up Initiative, from April to June. This campaign includes various activities such as public talks, art exhibitions, and social media promotions aimed at raising awareness about environmental issues affecting Easter Island. Local artists contribute by creating works that highlight the beauty of the island and the importance of conservation, while public talks feature experts discussing topics related to environmental protection and cultural preservation. Social media campaigns extend the reach of the initiative beyond the island, engaging a global audience in the conversation about sustainable practices. Visitors can participate by attending events, sharing their experiences on social media, and spreading the message of conservation. The campaign is free to join, and its impact extends far beyond the island, inspiring a broader audience to support and engage in environmental stewardship. By participating in the Environmental Awareness Campaign, visitors not only contribute to the island's efforts but also become ambassadors for conservation on a global scale.

8.4 Cultural Heritage Day

Every August, the island hosts Cultural Heritage Day, a celebration dedicated to preserving and showcasing the island's unique heritage. This annual event is an immersive experience into the customs, arts, and traditions of the Rapa Nui people, offering visitors a rare opportunity to witness and participate in the island's cultural practices. Held in various locations across the island, Cultural Heritage Day is a testament to the enduring spirit of Rapa Nui's rich cultural legacy.

The Moai Carving Demonstrations: One of the most captivating events during Cultural Heritage Day is the Moai Carving Demonstrations. These workshops provide a fascinating glimpse into the ancient art of creating the iconic Moai statues that have made Easter Island famous. Held at the Rano Raraku quarry, where many of these statues were originally carved, the demonstrations offer visitors a chance to see artisans at work, using traditional tools and techniques passed down through generations. The quarry, located about a 30-minute drive from Hanga Roa, is accessible via guided tours that often include transportation from the town. The carving demonstrations are free to attend, though it is advisable to join a guided tour to fully appreciate the historical context and significance of the Moai statues. The artisans' skillful use of basalt and volcanic tuff to create these massive figures is not only a testament to their craftsmanship but also an insight into the spiritual and social importance of the Moai in Rapa Nui culture. Visitors to the carving demonstrations will be able to engage with the artisans, learn about the symbolic meanings behind the Moai, and gain a deeper appreciation for the island's artistic heritage. The experience is a profound connection to the island's past and a visual celebration of its continuing traditions.

Traditional Dance Performances: Another highlight of Cultural Heritage Day is the series of traditional dance performances held at the main square of Hanga Roa. The square becomes a vibrant stage where local dancers, dressed in elaborate costumes made of feathers, shells, and traditional textiles, perform dances that narrate the myths, legends, and daily life of the Rapa Nui people. These performances are a lively and colorful representation of Rapa Nui's oral history, with each dance telling a story that has been passed down through generations. The dances are accompanied by traditional music played on drums and wooden instruments, creating a rhythmic and hypnotic experience. The square is easily accessible from most accommodations in Hanga Roa, making it a convenient location for visitors to immerse themselves in the island's cultural expressions. The dance performances are open to the public with no entry fee, though seating can be limited. Arriving early will ensure a good view and allow visitors to enjoy the pre-show festivities, where they can interact with locals and learn about the significance of the dances. The performances offer a vibrant and emotional connection to the island's cultural heritage, making them a must-see during Cultural Heritage Day.

The Rapa Nui Cuisine Festival: The Rapa Nui Cuisine Festival is a gastronomic event that takes place at Anakena Beach, one of the island's most picturesque locations. Held as part of Cultural Heritage Day, this festival showcases the traditional dishes of the Rapa Nui people, offering visitors a taste of the island's culinary heritage. The festival features a range of dishes prepared using traditional methods and ingredients, including seafood, root vegetables, and fruits that are native to the island. Anakena Beach, known for its stunning white sand and clear waters, is the perfect backdrop for this culinary celebration. The festival is free to attend, though visitors should budget for food and beverages, as local vendors offer a variety of traditional dishes for purchase. The experience of enjoying Rapa Nui cuisine with the ocean as a backdrop creates a memorable and immersive cultural experience. Visitors to the Rapa Nui Cuisine Festival can explore food stalls offering everything from fresh seafood to traditional dishes like "umù," a dish cooked in an underground oven. The festival also provides opportunities to learn about the traditional cooking methods and the cultural significance of various ingredients. This event is a delightful way to engage with Rapa Nui culture through its rich and diverse culinary traditions.

The Traditional Craft Fair: The Traditional Craft Fair, held at the island's cultural center in Hanga Roa, is a vibrant display of Rapa Nui craftsmanship. This event features local artisans showcasing their skills in making traditional crafts such as woven baskets, feathered ornaments, and intricate wood carvings. The fair is an opportunity for visitors to purchase authentic Rapa Nui souvenirs while supporting local artists and preserving traditional craft techniques. Located in the heart of Hanga Roa, the cultural center is easily accessible and provides a hub for the island's artistic community. The craft fair is open to the public with no entry fee, making it an accessible and enriching experience for all visitors. The fair also includes live demonstrations where artisans explain their techniques and the cultural significance of their crafts. Attending the Traditional Craft Fair allows visitors to gain a deeper understanding of Rapa Nui art forms and their role in daily life. Engaging with the artisans and exploring their creations offers a personal connection to the island's cultural heritage, making it a valuable and memorable part of Cultural Heritage Day.

The Ancestral Games: The Ancestral Games are a series of traditional competitions held at the sports field near Hanga Roa, showcasing the physical prowess and cultural knowledge of the Rapa Nui people. These games include activities such as spear throwing, coconut husking races, and traditional wrestling, each reflecting skills that were historically important for survival and community life on the island. The sports field, located a short distance from the main town, is transformed into a lively arena where locals and visitors alike can witness these traditional competitions. The games are free to watch, though visitors should check the schedule in advance to ensure they don't miss any of the action. Participating in or watching the Ancestral Games provides a fascinating insight into Rapa Nui's cultural values and community spirit. The games are a celebration of physical strength, agility, and traditional skills, offering a dynamic and engaging experience that highlights the island's rich heritage.

8.5 Christmas on Easter Island

Christmas on Easter Island is a distinctive experience that intertwines traditional holiday festivities with the island's unique cultural heritage. Celebrated in December, this period is marked by a series of events that blend local customs with festive cheer, creating a holiday experience unlike any other. The island, renowned for its enigmatic Moai statues and breathtaking landscapes, becomes a vibrant tapestry of celebration during this time. From traditional island feasts to community gatherings and Christmas concerts, each event offers a glimpse into how Easter Islanders infuse global holiday traditions with their own cultural practices.

Nochebuena: Nochebuena, or Christmas Eve, is a highlight of the Christmas season on Easter Island, held on the evening of December 24th. The celebration takes place in Hanga Roa, the island's main town, where locals and visitors gather for a festive evening filled with traditional music, dance, and communal feasting. The festivities often begin with a midnight Mass at the local church, where the community comes together to celebrate the birth of Christ in a service that combines Catholic traditions with local customs. Following the Mass, the town square comes alive with music and dance performances, showcasing the island's vibrant cultural heritage. Traditional dishes such as roast meats, fresh seafood, and tropical fruits are served, reflecting a blend of local ingredients and festive fare. Visitors are welcome to join in the celebrations, which are free of charge but may involve contributions to communal food preparations. The event offers a warm and welcoming atmosphere, allowing visitors to experience the island's unique blend of Christmas traditions and local culture.

Christmas Day Festival: Christmas Day on Easter Island is celebrated with a festival that spans the entire day, from December 25th. The main events are centered around the town of Hanga Roa, where the community comes together for a series of activities that include traditional games, music, and a communal barbecue. The festival is held in various locations around the town, including the central plaza and local parks. Visitors can enjoy performances by local musicians and dancers, participate in traditional games, and sample a range of festive foods. The highlight of the day is the communal barbecue, where families and friends gather to share meals and enjoy each other's company. Entry to the festival is free, although visitors are encouraged to bring along a dish or drink to share with others, enhancing the communal spirit of the event. The Christmas Day Festival is a wonderful opportunity to experience the island's festive spirit and engage with the local community in a joyous and inclusive celebration.

Terevaka Christmas Concert: In late December, the Terevaka Christmas Concert is a prominent event that showcases the island's musical talent and cultural fusion. Held at the Terevaka Cultural Center in Hanga Roa, this concert features performances by local musicians and dancers, blending traditional Rapa Nui music with contemporary holiday tunes. The concert is a vibrant display of the island's artistic heritage, offering a unique interpretation of Christmas music that incorporates traditional instruments and rhythms. Attendees can expect a lively and engaging performance, with opportunities to join in traditional dances and sing along to familiar carols with a local twist. The Terevaka Christmas Concert typically has an entry fee, which helps support the cultural center and its ongoing programs. Visitors are advised to purchase tickets in advance, as the concert often attracts a full house. This event provides a captivating insight into the island's musical traditions and the creative ways in which local artists celebrate the holiday season.

Cultural Workshops and Craft Fairs: During the Christmas season, Easter Island hosts a series of cultural workshops and craft fairs that offer visitors a chance to engage with local artisans and learn about traditional crafts. These events, held throughout December, take place in various locations including community centers and local markets. The workshops focus on traditional Rapa Nui crafts such as weaving, carving, and painting, providing visitors with hands-on experiences and the opportunity to create their own souvenirs. The craft fairs feature stalls selling handmade items, including intricate wood carvings, colorful textiles, and traditional jewelry. Visitors can interact with local artisans, gain insight into their techniques, and purchase unique gifts that reflect the island's cultural heritage. Entry to the craft fairs is typically free, with costs associated with purchasing crafts or participating in workshops. These events offer a meaningful way to connect with the island's artistic traditions and support local craftspeople during the holiday season.

INSIDER TIPS AND RECOMMENDATIONS

To fully appreciate and experience the island's unique charm, a few insider tips can transform your journey from merely memorable to truly extraordinary. Here's a guide to help you unlock the best of Easter Island, ensuring that your visit is as immersive and unforgettable as it should be.

Embrace the Island's Pace and Spirit: Easter Island is known for its serene and laid-back atmosphere, a stark contrast to the hustle and bustle of many travel destinations. One of the best pieces of advice for any visitor is to embrace this slower pace. The island's charm lies in its relaxed vibe, so take the time to soak in the tranquility, whether you're exploring ancient sites, enjoying a beach sunset, or conversing with the locals. Allow yourself to disconnect from the fast pace of modern life and reconnect with the island's timeless rhythm. This attitude will enhance your experience, helping you appreciate the subtleties of Rapa Nui culture and natural beauty.

Explore Beyond the Moai: While the Moai statues are undoubtedly the island's most famous attraction, Easter Island offers much more than just these monumental figures. For a truly immersive experience, venture beyond the well-trodden paths. Discover the lesser-known archaeological sites, such as the hidden Ahu Akivi, which features seven Moai gazing out towards the ocean, reflecting a unique aspect of Rapa Nui's history and culture. Hike to the volcanic craters of Rano Kau and Rano Raraku, where you can marvel at the Moai quarry and gain insight into the statue-carving process. These excursions offer a deeper understanding of the island's heritage and provide stunning vistas away from the more crowded tourist spots.

Engage with the Local Community: One of the most rewarding aspects of visiting Easter Island is the opportunity to engage with its local community. The Rapa Nui people are known for their warmth and hospitality, and interacting with them can provide a richer, more authentic experience. Attend local cultural events, such as the Tapati Festival or traditional dance performances, where you can learn firsthand about the island's traditions and folklore. Don't hesitate to ask locals about their stories, customs, and daily life—many are eager to share their heritage with curious visitors. Engaging with the community not only enriches your understanding of Rapa Nui culture but also fosters meaningful connections that will stay with you long after you leave the island.

Pack Wisely and Respectfully: Easter Island's remote location means that services and supplies can be limited, so packing wisely is essential. Bring sturdy walking shoes for exploring the rugged terrain, sun protection including hats and sunscreen, and lightweight clothing suitable for both warm days and cooler evenings. Also, be mindful of local customs and dress modestly when visiting sacred sites. Respecting the island's cultural norms not only shows consideration but also helps you gain the respect and goodwill of the local community. Additionally, consider packing reusable water bottles and bags to minimize your environmental impact, as the island's ecosystem is fragile and requires careful stewardship.

Plan for a Digital Detox: Easter Island's isolation offers a unique chance to disconnect from the digital world and fully immerse yourself in the island's natural beauty and cultural experiences. Many visitors find that a temporary digital detox enhances their enjoyment and engagement with the island. While Wi-Fi is available in some areas, connectivity can be spotty, which presents a perfect opportunity to unplug and focus on the moment. Use this time to explore the island's landscapes, engage with local traditions, and create meaningful memories without the distractions of everyday life. This approach will allow you to experience the island's true essence and connect more deeply with its people and environment.

Respect the Sacred Sites: The Moai statues and other archaeological sites on Easter Island are not just tourist attractions but sacred symbols of the Rapa Nui culture. It is crucial to approach these sites with respect and reverence. Follow all posted guidelines and avoid touching or climbing on the Moai statues and other ancient structures. Always stay on marked paths and trails to protect both the sites and the environment. By respecting these guidelines, you help preserve the island's heritage for future generations and honor the cultural significance of these remarkable monuments.

Engage in Local Cuisine: Exploring Easter Island's culinary offerings is an essential part of experiencing its culture. While the island's cuisine may not be as widely known as its historical sites, it offers unique flavors and dishes that reflect the local environment and traditions. Try traditional Rapa Nui dishes such as "umù," a feast cooked in an underground oven, or fresh seafood caught from the surrounding waters. Visiting local markets and eateries will provide a taste of island life and a deeper appreciation for the Rapa Nui way of living.

Engaging with local cuisine is not just about eating; it's about connecting with the culture and savoring the island's flavors.

Respect the Environment: Easter Island's delicate ecosystem requires careful consideration from all visitors. The island's environment is fragile, with unique flora and fauna that can be easily disrupted. Follow the principles of "leave no trace" by avoiding littering and staying on designated paths. Support conservation efforts by participating in eco-friendly tours and activities that prioritize the protection of the island's natural resources. By being a responsible traveler, you contribute to the preservation of Easter Island's beauty and help ensure that future generations can enjoy its wonders.

Easter Island is a destination that offers more than just awe-inspiring Moai statues; it's a place where ancient traditions, vibrant culture, and natural beauty come together in a unique and unforgettable way. By following these insider tips, you can enhance your visit, immerse yourself in the island's rich heritage, and create lasting memories. Your journey to this remote paradise will be a profound and enriching adventure, offering insights and experiences that will linger long after you return home.

Made in the USA
Columbia, SC
21 April 2025